KENTUCKY

REVISED AND EXPANDED EDITION

GOLF

Kentucky Golf *The Complete Guide to Golfing in the Bluegrass.*

Design and publishing services:
  Butler Book Publishing Services, Inc., Louisville, Kentucky

Cover Illustrator:
  Chris Brauckmann Ewalt

Although the author and publisher have exhaustively researched all sources to ensure the accuracy and completeness of the information contained in this book, we assume no responsibility for errors, omissions or any inconsistency herein. The publisher welcomes any new or updated information.

Kentucky Golf is a Trademark ™ of
  Stoneham Communications, Inc.
  P. O. Box 6603
  Louisville, Kentucky 40207

Kentucky Golf, Inc. is a Sponsor Member of the National Golf Foundation.

ISBN 0-9625904-5-2

Printed and bound in the United States of America.

This book is dedicated to

Laurie and Lee

ACKNOWLEDGEMENTS

Mike Donahue, PGA, Executive Director Kentucky
Section, Profesional Golf Association, and Maria
Temprano for helping us to start with this project.

The excellent staff at Butler Book Publishing Services,
Inc. for their tireless efforts to make the new *Kentucky
Golf* possible.

The Directors of Andry Montgomery, Inc. for encouragement to follow through.

John Rood, founder of "Better Golf for Everyone"
Lexington, Kentucky, for insight to the growing and
important role of the Stand Alone Range and Alternative Golf Facility.

Very special gratitude is expressed to the thousands of
fans of the first version, *Kentucky Golf, 1990 Edition*
and to Mr. Gene Gardner of Louisville for helping to
make that first effort a reality.

TABLE OF CONTENTS

INTRODUCTION

What's New

When the first edition of *Kentucky Golf* was published in 1990, we profiled and listed a total of 208 golf courses. This revised and updated edition has been expanded significantly. The pages that follow are packed with need-to-know information about 219 regulation courses, 11 par-three and 9 executive complexes, and 7 practice ranges.

You now have access to a total of 246 golfing facilities, including a variety of new challenges that have popped up around the state. Did you know, for example, that Kentucky has a course that offers 54 holes of rigorous play, one 36-hole arena and three sites where you have a choice of three 9-hole layouts? Looking at it another way, Kentucky gives you 3,195 different opportunities to test your skills, wits and scores. And those are just the regulation holes!

We are indeed blessed with a wealth of golfing resources throughout the Commonwealth.

New Organization

Friends and advisors suggested that *Kentucky Golf* itself might be laid out differently. Instead of arranging the book by cities, we were told it would be helpful to look at golfing opportunities region by region. We agreed.

Therefore the state and its golf courses have been separated into four regions: North Central, Eastern, South Central and Western.

New Alternatives

It was also suggested that we include so-called "Alternative Golf Facilities." Again, we agreed, and you will find a listing of the practice ranges, par-three and executive courses at the end of each Regional Section.

What's Not New

There are still some "ghost courses" in this edition, facilities that we were unable to profile for one reason or another. Last time we had 53; this book has only 31, mostly private country clubs that are not open to the public anyway. Nonetheless, we want our readers to have a peek at all of Kentucky's finest. We will continue to try to obtain information about these facilities for future editions. Meanwhile, end-of-section listings will have to do for now. (If your course has received only a listing, talk to your pro!)

New Views

And we are most pleased that this *Kentucky Golf* features illustrations of many of the courses. The wonders of publishing technology have come within our reach! We know you'll find these graphics interesting and helpful in assessing the difficulty and challenge of play.

What's Too New

Now for the disclaimers. Every effort has been made to provide the most current and accurate information. But things do change, without notice. If you're playing the course for the first time, it's a good idea to call ahead.

Thanks to Everyone

Once again, we want to thank all the people who have helped make *Kentucky Golf* happen. We are grateful to the many PGA pros, club and pro shop managers and even course superintendents who gave us new insights into the playing fields of Kentucky.

We hope this edition will help you get more out of your game and your Kentucky links.

> Lane Stoneham
> Editor
> Kentucky Golf,
> Louisville, Kentucky, USA

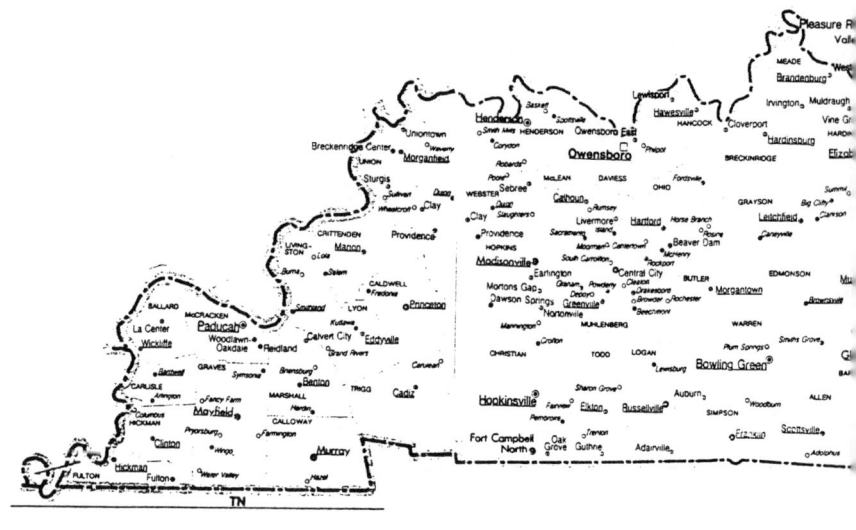

Map of the Commonwealth of Kentucky

NORTH CENTRAL

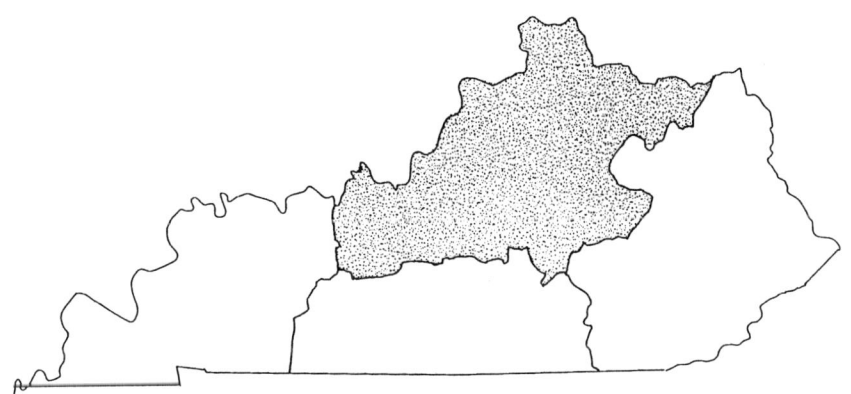

A. J. Jolly Golf Course

5350 U. S. 27
Alexandria, Kentucky
606-635-2106

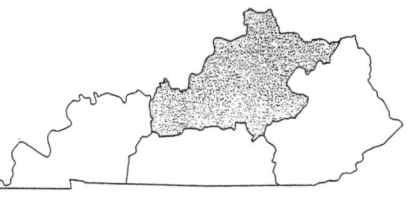

Location – Six miles south of Alexandria on U. S. 27.

Public	
Year Round – 18 Holes	
Pro – Terry Jolly	

Greens Fees Guests

Weekdays	$12.00
Evenings	$7.00
Weekends	$12.00

Facilities/Services Available
Pro Shop • Putting Green •
Chipping Green • Snack Bar •
Meeting Room • Dressing
Rooms (M & W) • Showers (M) •
Private Lockers (M) • Golf
Lessons • Club Repair • Group
Play • Memberships

Rental Equipment

	9 holes	18 holes
Carts	$9.00	$16.00
Pull Carts	$.50	$1.00
Golf Clubs	$3.00	$3.00

Course Description – This scenic course has water everywhere! Lakes intersect 7, 8, 15 and 17, while fairways on 10
and 18 are lined by still more water.

1992 Champions –
Men's – Tony Pfefferman
Women's – Carol Havlin

Tees:	Blue	White	Red
PAR:	71	71	75
Yardage:	6183	5805	5381
Rating:	69.3	67.6	70.3
Slope Rating:	118	115	118

Owl Creek Country Club

12400 Osage Road
Anchorage, Kentucky
502-245-4156

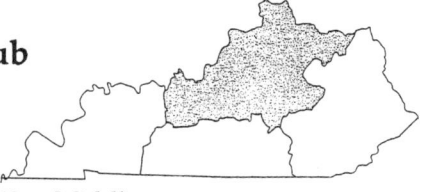

Location – Two miles off U. S. 60 at Middletown.

Private
Year Round – 9 Holes
Pro – Joe Lally, Jr., PGA

Greens Fees Guests
Weekdays $18.00
Weekends $25.00

Facilities/Services Available
Pro Shop • Driving Range •
Putting Green • Chipping
Green • Practice Bunker •
Snack Bar • Dining Room •
Lounge • Meeting Room •
Dressing Rooms (M & W) •
Showers (M & W) • Private
Lockers (M & W) • Golf
Lessons • Club Repair •
Memberships

Rental Equipment

	9 holes	18 holes
Carts	$10.00	$18.00
Pull Carts	$2.00	$2.00

Course Description – Tight, tree-lined fairways characterize
this course, nestled in a Louisville suburb. Creeks cross
fairways on three holes, and bunkers increase challenge
throughout, as do small greens.

1992 Champions –
Men's – Andy Walker   Senior – C. L. Boden
Women's – Alice Boden

Tees:	Blue/White	Red/White
PAR:	71	74
Yardage:	6137	5695
Rating:	67.4	70.4
Slope Rating:	109	114

Cedar-Fil Golf Course

2330 New Shepherdsville Road
Bardstown, Kentucky
502-348-8981

Location – Two and one-half miles northwest of town on
Highway 245.

Public
Year Round – 18 Holes
Manager – Roger Filiatreau

Greens Fees
Weekdays $8.00
Weekends $10.00

Facilities/Services Available
Pro Shop • Putting Green •
Snack Bar

Rental Equipment

	9 holes	18 holes
Carts	$10.00	$16.00
Pull Carts	$1.00	$1.00
Golf Clubs	$2.00	$2.00

Course Description – Tree-lined, flat terrain is easy to walk.
The most difficult hole is no. 15, a 393-yard par 4.

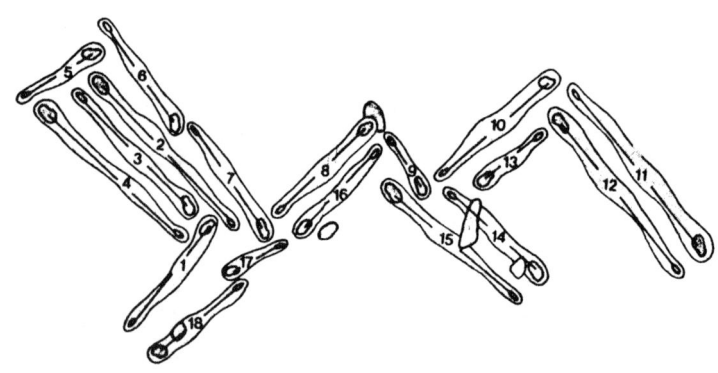

Tees:	Blue	White	Red
PAR:	72		72
Yardage:	5938		5233

My Old Kentucky Home Country Club

My Old Kentucky Home State Park
Bardstown, Kentucky
502-349-6542

Location – Bluegrass Parkway to U. S. 31E and Highway 150.

Public

Year Round – 18 Holes

Manager – Joan Rizer

Greens Fees
Weekdays $15.00
Weekends $15.00
Golf Card is accepted.
Kentucky State Parks pass program.

Facilities/Services Available
Pro Shop •Driving Range •
Putting Green • Chipping
Green • Snack Bar • Dressing
Rooms (M & W) • Showers (M
& W) • Private Lockers (M) •
Club Repair • Group Play •
Memberships

Rental Equipment

	9 holes	18 holes
Carts	$9.00	$17.00

Course Description – The "Home of the Kentucky Bourbon Open" is located on the grounds behind historic Old Kentucky Home. Large wooded areas tighten fairways, while small greens test short skills. New 9 holes are part of this challenging course.

1992 Champions –
Men's – Jimmy Mattingly   Senior – Jerry Werner
Women's– A. J. Burba

Tees:	Blue	White	Red
PAR:	70	70	70
Yardage:	6065	5796	5239
Rating:	69.5	68.3	70.2
Slope Rating:	119	117	118

Deer Run Golf Course

Route 2, Starks Lane
Bedford, Kentucky
502-255-7770

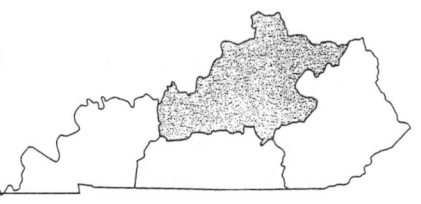

Location – About one mile south of Bedford off 421 on Starks Lane.

Public

Year Round – 9 Holes

Owner – Roy L. Winchester

Greens Fees
Weekdays $7.00
Weekends $9.00

Facilities/Services Available
Pro Shop • Putting Green •
Snack Bar • Group Play •
Memberships

Rental Equipment

	9 holes	18 holes
Carts	$6.50	$13.00
Pull Carts	$1.00	$1.00
Golf Clubs	$2.00	$2.00

Course Description – Trees complicate the game throughout the course, as does water on three holes.

1992 Champions –
Men's – Ronnie Booth
Women's – Sarah Floyd

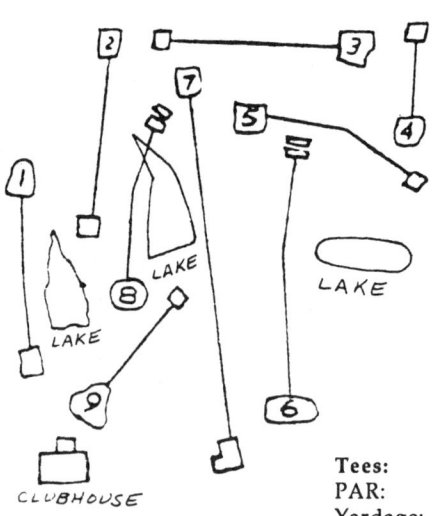

Tees:	Blue	White	Red
PAR:	36	36	36
Yardage:	3215	3035	2855

Berea Country Club

Lorraine Court
Berea, Kentucky
606-986-3078

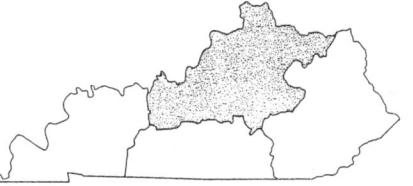

Location – Behind Churchill Weavers in downtown Berea.

Semi-Private	
Year Round – 9 Holes	
Pro – Ned McAfee, PGA	

Greens Fees Public/Guests
Weekday $12.00 / $12.00
Weekends $15.00 / $15.00

Facilities/Services Available
  Pro Shop • Meeting Room •
  Dressing Rooms (M & W) •
  Showers (M & W) • Private
  Lockers (M & W) • Golf
  Lessons • Club Repair •
  Group Play • Memberships

Rental Equipment

	9 holes	18 holes
Carts	$7.00	$14.00
Pull Carts	$2.00	$2.00

Course Description – Trees, water and bunkers add lively variety to this golf-scape. Keen strategy is required on the 485-yard no. 5, where a stream snakes throughout.

1992 Champions –
Men's – Mark Cox
Women's – Jeanie White

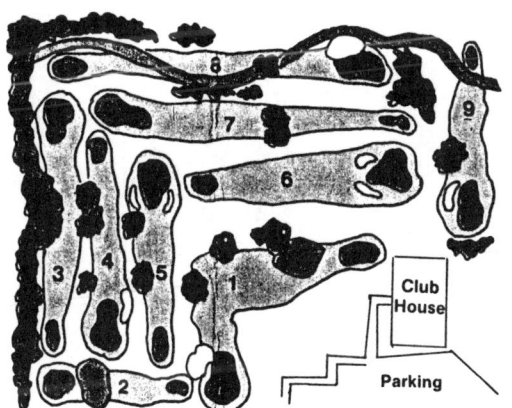

Tees:	Blue	Red
PAR:	36	37
Yardage:	2914	2573

Doe Valley Country Club

Highway 1638
Brandenburg, Kentucky
502-422-3397

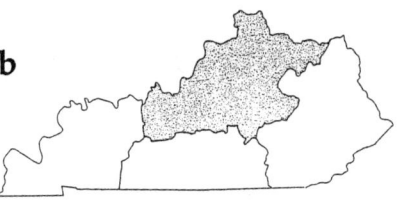

Location – Thirty-five minutes south of Louisville, just off Highway 31W.

Semi-Private

Closed January – 18 Holes

Pro – Marc Williams, PGA

Greens Fees

Weekdays $12.00
Weekends $17.00

Facilities/Services Available
Pro Shop • Putting Green •
Snack Bar • Dining Room •
Lounge • Meeting Room •
Golf Lessons • Club Repair •
Group Play • Memberships •
Outings

Rental Equipment

	9 holes	18 holes
Carts	$9.00	$16.00

Course Description – Rolling hills feature tree-lined fairways. The course difficulty increases thanks to four water hazards. Ranked among *Business First's* Top 12 Kentucky Golf Courses.

1992 Champions –
Men's – Jerry Garris
Women's – Anne Pace

| 1 | 2 | 3 | 4 | 5 | 6 | 7 | 8 | 9 | 10 | 11 | 12 |

| 13 | 14 | 15 | 16 | 17 | 18 |

Tees:	Blue	White	Red
PAR:	71	71	72
Yardage:	6471	6196	5519
Rating:	69.8	68.3	70.3
Slope Rating:	119	116	118

Hillcrest Country Club
Brandenburg, Kentucky
502-422-4455

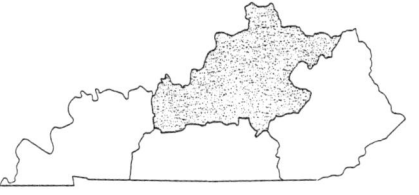

Location – Off Kentucky State 220.

Semi-Private
Year Round – 9 Holes

Greens Fees Guests
Weekday $8.00
Weekends $10.00

Facilities/Services Available
Pro Shop • Putting Green •
Chipping Green • Snack Bar •
Dining Room • Group Play •
Memberships

Rental Equipment

	9 holes	18 holes
Carts	$9.00	$14.00

Course Description – Hilly, wooded, challenging. No. 5 is a long par 5.

Tees:	Blue	White	Red
PAR:	36	36	36

L & N Golf Club
Highway 1020
Brooks, Kentucky
502-955-9987

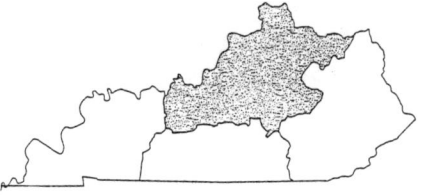

Location – One-half mile south of Jefferson County line on Highway 1020.

Private
Year Round – 18 Holes
Manager – John Harp

Greens Fees Guests
Weekday $10.00
Weekends $23.00

Facilities/Services Available
Pro Shop • Putting Green •
Snack Bar • Dressing Rooms
(M & W) • Showers (M & W) •
Private Lockers (M & W) •
Memberships

Rental Equipment

	9 holes	18 holes
Carts	$6.00	$12.00
Pull Carts	$.50	$1.00

Course Description – The front nine is moderately hilly, while the back side is rolling. The green is a difficult target on the 483-yard 5th hole as it is guarded by lakes in front and back. These links are tree-lined and well-bunkered.

Tees:	Blue	Red
PAR:	71	71
Yardage:	6143	5269
Rating:	68.7	67.1
Slope Rating:	121	117

Meadowood Golf Cub
5353 Limaburg Road
Burlington, Kentucky
606-371-8621

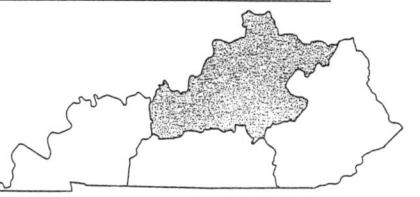

Location – Four miles south of Greater Cincinnati Airport.

Public	
Year Round – 18 Holes	
Pro –Danny Woods, PGA	

Greens Fees
Weekdays $14.50
Weekends $14.50

Facilities/Services Available
Pro Shop • Putting Green •
Chipping Green • Snack Bar •
Lounge • Dressing Rooms (M
& W) •Private Lockers (M & W)
• Golf Lessons • Club Repair
• Group Play

Rental Equipment

	9 holes	18 holes
Carts	$11.00	$19.00
Pull Carts	$1.50	$1.50

Course Description – Rolling, easy-to-walk course is appealing for ladies and seniors. Water makes for tricky play on 10, 11 and 13. Over the next five years, total renovation is planned.

1992 Champions –
Men's – Ron Foltz
Women's – Kim Gunning

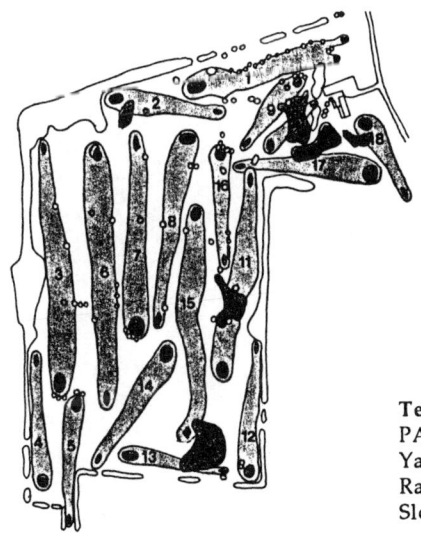

Tees:	White	Red
PAR:	69	66
Yardage:	5130	4327
Rating:	62.3	63.4
Slope Rating:	100	101

Traditions Golf Course
2035 Williams Road
Burlington, Kentucky
606-586-6691

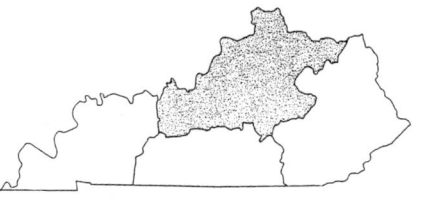

Location

Private
18 Holes
Pro – Jim Stockwell

Greens Fees
Weekdays $25.00
Weekends $35.00

Facilities/Services Available
Pro Shop • Driving Range •
Putting Green • Chipping
Green • Practice Bunker •
Snack Bar • Golf Lessons •
Club Repair • Memberships

Course Description – Traditions Golf Course has 18 holes of
challenging, beautiful golf that rambles over 400 acres of
some of the most dramatic land in Northern Kentucky.

1992 Champions –
Men's – Jim Volpenhein

Tees:	Blue	Red
PAR:	72	72
Yardage:	7068	6464
Rating:	73.3	71.0
Slope Rating:	136	127

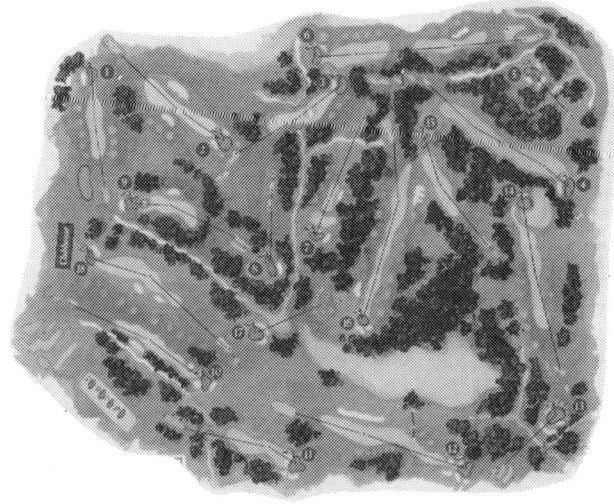

General Butler State Resort Park

Highway 227
Carrollton, Kentucky
502-732-4384

Location – I-71 N to Highway 227.

Public
Year Round – 9 Holes
Manager – John Nicholson

Greens Fees
Weekdays $10.00
Evenings $10.00
Weekends $10.00

Facilities/Services Available
Pro Shop • Putting Green •
Snack Bar • Dining Room •
Lounge •

Rental Equipment

	9 holes	18 holes
Carts	$9.00	$17.00
Pull Carts	$1.00	$1.00
Golf Clubs	$5.00	$5.00

Course Description – Hilly, wooded terrain is not well-suited for walking. Variety demands both concentration and prowess.

Tees:	Blue	White	Red
PAR:	70	70	72
Yardage:	2820	2700	2465

Meadows Golf Course
Clay City, Kentucky
606-663-4000

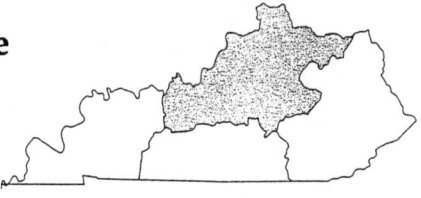

Location – North of Clay City on Fife Lick Road.

Public	**Greens Fees**
9 Holes	Weekdays $3.00
Owner – Roscoe Meadows	Weekends $4.00

Facilities/Services Available
Pro Shop • Putting Green •
Snack Bar • Chipping Green •
Group Play

Rental Equipment

	9 holes	18 holes
Carts	$5.30	$10.60

Course Description –Flat, open.

Tees:	Blue
PAR:	36
Yardage:	2845

Devou Park Golf & Tennis Club

1344 Audubon Road
Covington, Kentucky
606-431-8030

Location – I-75 Western Lane exit to Audubon Road.

Public
Year Round – 9 Holes
Pro – Ralph Landrum, PGA

Greens Fees

	9 Holes	18 Holes
Weekdays	$7.50	$12.50

Facilities/Services Available
Pro Shop • Driving Range •
Putting Green • Chipping
Green • Snack Bar • Dining
Room • Lounge • Meeting
Room • Dressing Rooms (M) •
Showers (M) • Private
Lockers (M) • Golf Lessons •
Club Repair • Group Play •
Memberships

Rental Equipment

	9 holes	18 holes
Carts	$11.00	$18.00
Pull Carts	$2.00	$2.00
Golf Clubs	$2.00	$2.00

Course Description – Scenic rolling hills are placed in the middle of a 700-acre park. This course overlooks the Ohio River.

Tees:	Blue	White	Red
PAR:	36	36	36
Yardage:	2740	2610	2046
Rating:	71.4	70.1	69.7
Slope Rating:	123	120	117

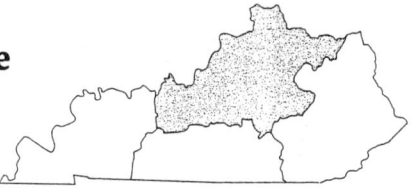

Twin Oaks Golf Course

43rd & Michigan Ave.
Covington, Kentucky
606-581-2410

Location – Exit 79 off I-275; right on Church Street, right on 43rd.

Public
March thru December – 18 Holes
Owner – Susie Swingos-Hilliard

Greens Fees

	9 Holes	18 Holes
Weekdays	$8.00	$13.00
Senior rates before noon		
M - F –	$6.00	$9.00

Facilities/Services Available
Pro Shop • Putting Green •
Snack Bar • Dining Room •
Lounge • Meeting Room •
Dressing Rooms (M& W) •
Showers (M) • Golf Lessons •
Club Repair • Group Play •

Rental Equipment

	9 holes	18 holes
Carts	$10.50	$18.50
Pull Carts	$1.00	$1.50
Golf Clubs	$5.00	$5.00

Course Description – Wide, tree-lined fairways built on 162 acres of fertile ground make for a challenge to the better golfer while allowing the average golfer a pleasurable round. Newly added lakes, elevated tees and greens, along with 18 holes of cart paths and 66 brand new E-Z Go carts, make for an enjoyable round.

1992 Champions –
Men's – Dave Macke   Senior – Jim Ryle
Women's – Rita Schawe   Junior – John Fangmeyer

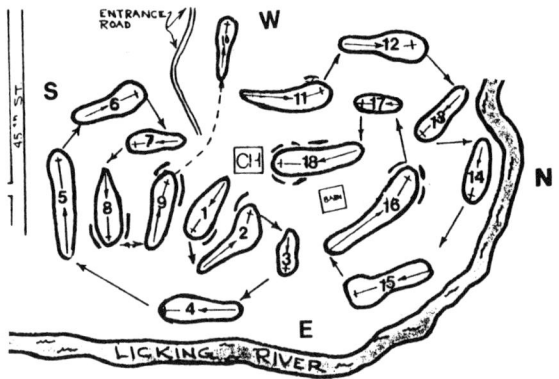

Tees:	Blue	White	Red
PAR:	70	70	70
Yardage:	6406	6112	5305
Rating:	70.0	68.7	70.1
Slope Rating:	112	109	111

Summit Hills Country Club
236 Dudley
Crestview Hills, Kentucky
606-341-7799

Location – 275 E to Turkeyfoot exit, turn right for 1-1/2 miles to Dudley.

Private	Greens Fees Guests	
Year Round – 18 Holes	Weekdays	$20.00
Pro – John Steinbrunner, PGA	Weekends	$30.00

Facilities/Services Available
Pro Shop • Driving Range •
Putting Green • Chipping Green
• Practice Bunker • Snack Bar •
Dining Room • Lounge •
Meeting Room • Dressing
Rooms (M & W) • Showers (M
& W) • Private Lockers (M &
W) • Golf Lessons • Club
Repair • Group Play • Member-
ships

Rental Equipment

	9 holes	18 holes
Carts	$10.00	$18.00
Pull Carts	$1.00	$1.50

Course Description – This rolling layout has narrow fairways and two lakes which punish wayward strokes. For the most part, holes are straight and of medium length.

1992 Champions –
Men's – Phil Wehrman
Women's – Dot Bankemper
Senior – Ed Park
Junior – Tom Goecke

Tees:	Blue	White	Red
PAR:	70	70	71
Yardage:	6296	6021	5352
Rating:	69.0	68.4	70.0
Slope Rating:	115	112	131

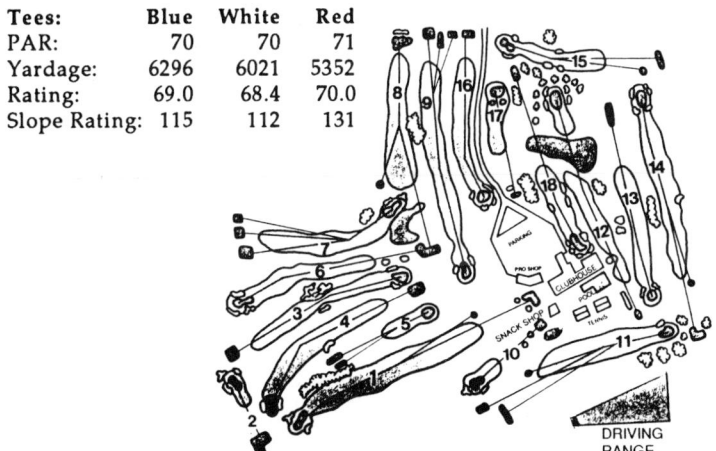

DRIVING
RANGE

Cynthiana Country Club

Route 7
Cynthiana, Kentucky
606-234-5364

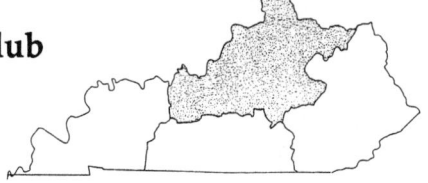

Location – Three miles southeast of U. S. 27.

Private

Closed January – 9 Holes

Golf Director – Paul Ewalt

Greens Fees Guests
Weekdays $10.00
Weekends $14.00

Facilities/Services Available
Pro Shop • Driving Range •
Putting Green • Chipping
Green • Snack Bar • Dining
Room • Lounge • Dressing
Rooms (M & W) • Showers (M &
W) • Private Lockers (M & W) •
Golf Lessons • Club Repair •
Group Play • Memberships

Rental Equipment

	9 holes	18 holes
Carts	$4.00	$7.00

Course Description A short field, this course has its perils. Woods and tight fairways wander through hills and valleys. Lake is on 2 and 7, with lateral water hazards near remaining holes.

1992 Champions –
Men's – Mike Lenox
Women's – Bonnie Whalen

Tees:	Blue	Red
PAR:	36	36
Yardage:	2861	2359
Rating:	67.7	66.7
Slope Rating:	120	114

Danville Country Club
Lexington Road
Danville, Kentucky
606-236-2838

Location – Four miles south of Highway 127.

Private
Year Round – 18 Holes
Pro – Mike Bibb, PGA

Greens Fees Guests
Weekdays $25.00
Evenings $25.00
Weekends $25.00

Facilities/Services Available
Pro Shop • Driving Range •
Putting Green • Snack Bar •
Dining Room • Dressing
Rooms (M & W) • Showers (M
& W) • Golf Lessons • Club
Repair • Memberships

Rental Equipment

	9 holes	18 holes
Carts	$8.00	$14.00

Course Description – Accuracy is required off the tee, with elevated approach shots into medium to small putting surfaces. Water hazards come into play on six holes.

1992 Champions –
Men's – Mike Kehoe

Women's – Judy Jackson

Senior – David Powell
Neal Gordon
Junior – Patrick McClure

Tees:	Blue	White	Red
PAR:	72	72	73
Yardage:	6680	6403	5297
Rating:	71.5	70.2	69.7
Slope Rating:	123	120	117

Old Bridge Golf Club
Old Bridge Road
Danville, Kentucky
606-236-6051

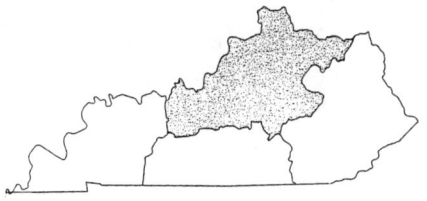

Location – Three miles east of Danville on Highway 84.

Semi-Private
Year Round – 9 Holes
Pro – Bruce A. Brown, PGA

Greens Fees Guests

Weekdays	$10.00
Evenings	$10.00
Weekends	$14.00

Facilities/Services Available
Pro Shop • Driving Range •
Putting Green • Snack Bar •
Golf Lessons • Club Repair •
Group Play • Memberships

Rental Equipment

	9 holes	18 holes
Carts	$4.00	$8.00
Pull Carts	$2.00	$3.00
Golf Clubs	$5.00	$5.00

Course Description – The course features rolling and natural terrain, with water on eight holes and some tight fairways.

Tees:	Blue	White
PAR:	36	36
Yardage:	3168	2854
Slope Rating:	116	115

Eagle Creek Country Club
Route 2
Dry Ridge, Kentucky
606-428-1772

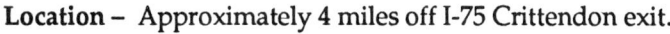

Location – Approximately 4 miles off I-75 Crittendon exit.

Semi-Private	**Greens Fees**
Closed January – 18 Holes	Weekdays $11.00
Pro – Doug Kenner	Weekends $13.00

Facilities/Services Available
Pro Shop • Putting Green •
Snack Bar • Meeting Room •
Dressing Rooms (M & W) •
Showers (M & W) • Private
Lockers (M) • Golf Lessons •
Club Repair • Group Play •
Memberships

Rental Equipment

	9 holes	18 holes
Carts	$8.00	$16.00
Pull Carts	$2.00	$3.00

Course Description – Doglegs and water are prominent
characteristics of this rolling course. Two lakes make play
intricate. A creek flows through 4, 9, 10, and 18, making each
complex.

1992 Champions –
Men's – Curtis Carpenter
Women's – Joyce Clemons

Tees:	Blue	White	Red
PAR:	70	70	71
Yardage:	5683	5683	5021
Rating:	69.0	67.1	66.9
Slope Rating:	111	109	109

Long Run Golf Course

Flat Rock Road
Eastwood, Kentucky
502-245-0702

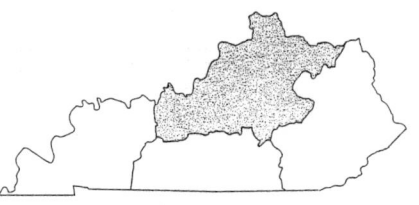

Location – In Eastwood off U. S. 60.

Public
Year Round – 18 Holes
Pro – Ken Diehlman, PGA

Greens Fees

Weekdays	$7.00
Weekends	$8.00
Pass programs available.	

Facilities/Services Available
Pro Shop • Driving Range •
Putting Green • Snack Bar •
Dressing Rooms (M & W) •
Showers (M & W) • Private
Lockers (M & W) • Golf
Lessons • Club Repair •
Group Play

Rental Equipment

	9 holes	18 holes
Carts	$10.00	$18.00
Pull Carts	$2.00	$2.00

Course Description – A versatile course that tests skills and accuracy, most holes are long and narrow. Water is a major factor on 8 and 15. Longest hole, 11, is a gruesome 560-yard 90-degree dogleg right.

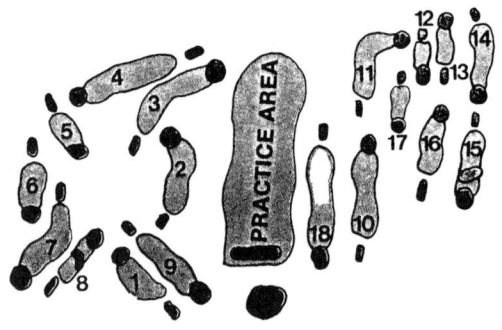

Tees:	Blue	White	Red
PAR:	72	72	73
Yardage:	6839	6584	5562
Rating:	71.5		71.4
Slope Rating:	113		111

Elizabethtown Country Club

2606 Hodgenville Road
Elizabethtown, Kentucky
502-737-7707

Location – Four miles east of I-65.

Private	
Year Round – 18 Holes	
Pro – Barry Fisher, PGA	

Greens Fees Guests
Weekdays $20.00
Weekends $20.00

Facilities/Services Available
  Pro Shop • Driving Range •
  Putting Green • Snack Bar •
  Dining Room • Meeting Room
  • Dressing Rooms (M & W) •
  Showers (M & W) • Private
  Lockers (M & W) • Golf
  Lessons • Club Repair •
  Group Play • Memberships

Rental Equipment

	9 holes	18 holes
Carts	$9.00	$17.00

Course Description – This well-conditioned course is laid out to test golfers of all abilities. Lakes and creeks complicate twelve holes! No. 18 is the most ferocious as a tree-lined, 566-yard dogleg left.

1992 Champions –
Men's – Rusty Horn
Women's – Kim Hartlage

Tees:	Blue	White	Red
PAR:	72	72	72
Yardage:	6617	6327	5616
Rating:	70.5	69.2	70.8
Slope Rating:	111	109	112

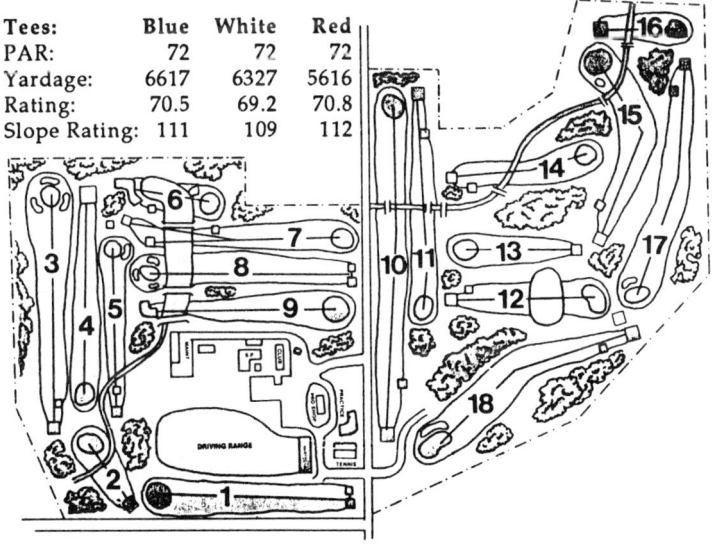

Pine Valley Country Club

850 Pine Valley Drive
Elizabethtown, Kentucky
502-737-8300

Location – One mile north of Elizabethtown Towne Mall off 31W.

Public **Year Round – 18 Holes** **Pro – Buddy Demling, PGA** **Course Manager – L. A. Medley**

Greens Fees
Weekdays　$12.00
Weekends　$17.00

Facilities/Services Available
Pro Shop • Driving Range • Putting Green • Chipping Green • Snack Bar •Dressing Rooms (M & W) • Golf Lessons • Club Repair • Group Play • Memberships

Rental Equipment

	18 holes
Carts	$18.00
Pull Carts	$2.00
Golf Clubs	$5.00

Course Description – The site of the Ben Hogan Elizabethtown Open provides a hearty challenge. Toughest test of skills comes on 2, a 622-yard double dogleg right. Water abounds, endangering seven holes.

Tees:	Blue	White	Red
PAR:	72	72	72
Yardage:	6753	6107	5411
Rating:	71.3	70.1	69.6
Slope Rating:	119	117	114

South Park Country Club

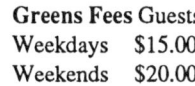

915 South Park Road
Fairdale, Kentucky
502-969-5757
Location – One mile south of Gene Snyder Freeway,
Fairdale exit.

Private
Year Round – 18 Holes
Pro – Bill Sullivan, PGA

Greens Fees Guests
Weekdays $15.00
Weekends $20.00

Facilities/Services Available
Pro Shop • Driving Range •
Putting Green • Chipping Green
• Practice Bunker • Snack Bar •
Dining Room • Lounge •
Meeting Room • Dressing
Rooms (M & W) • Showers (M &
W) • Private Lockers (M & W)
• Golf Lessons • Club Repair •
Group Play • Memberships

Rental Equipment

	9 holes	18 holes
Carts	$8.00	$16.00
Pull Carts	$2.00	$2.00

Course Description – This park-like course demands skills and
accuracy. Water figures prominently, appearing alongside 1,
16 and 17. Water must be crossed off 7th hole tee shot with
125-yard carry. Creek crosses 536-yard no. 8 in two places.
Trees engulf entire course.

1992 Champions –
Men's – Jerry Hard
Women's – Nancy Aldridge

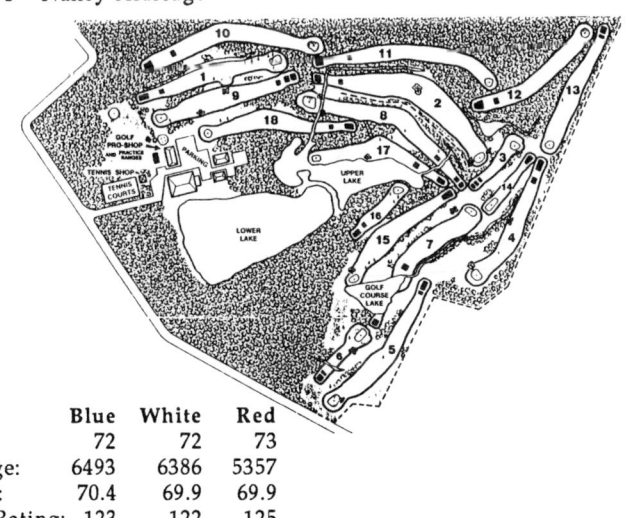

Tees:	Blue	White	Red
PAR:	72	72	73
Yardage:	6493	6386	5357
Rating:	70.4	69.9	69.9
Slope Rating:	123	122	125

Pendleton Country Club

Highway 27
Falmouth, Kentucky
606-472-2150

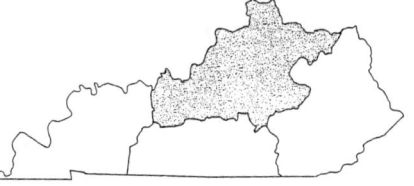

Location – Seven miles north of Falmouth on U. S. 27.

Private

March thru October – 9 Holes

Club Manager – Veta Bell

Greens Fees Guests
Weekdays $12.00
Weekends $15.00

Facilities/Services Available
Pro Shop • Driving Range •
Putting Green • Chipping
Green • Snack Bar • Dining
Room • Meeting Room •
Dressing Rooms (M & W) •
Showers (M & W) • Private
Lockers (M & W) • Member-
ships

Rental Equipment

	9 holes	18 holes
Carts	$4.00	$8.00
Pull Carts	$.50	

Course Description – Flat, open and short, this course has excellent tees, fairways and greens. Three water hazards factor into play.

1992 Champions –
Men's– Scott Young
Women's – Lisa Houchen

Tees:	Blue	Red
PAR:	36	37
Yardage:	3028	2624
Rating:	67.0	72.9
Slope Rating:	115	124

Fleming County Golf Association

Route 11
Flemingsburg, Kentucky
606-849-8161

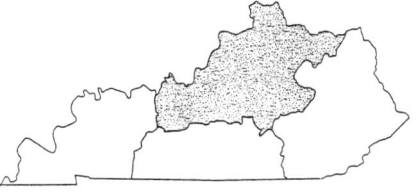

Location – One and one-half miles north of town on Route 11 North.

Semi-Private
Year Round – 9 Holes
Manager – Mike Dixon

Greens Fees

Weekdays	$4.00
Evenings	$4.00
Weekend	$5.00

Facilities/Services Available
Pro Shop • Driving Range • Putting Green • Chipping Green • Snack Bar • Meeting Room • Group Play • Memberships

Rental Equipment

	9 holes	18 holes
Carts	$3.50	$7.00
Pull Carts	$.50	$1.00

Course Description – A fairly open, hilly course, trees and creeks present the greatest threats on this layout.

Tees:	Blue	White	Red
PAR:	36	36	36
Yardage:	3017	2992	2902
Rating:	70.5		72.4
Slope Rating:	113		116

Boone Links

19 Clubhouse Drive
Florence, Kentucky
606-371-7550

Location – Two miles west of Florence Mall.

Public
Closed January – 27 Holes
Pro – Jeff Kruempelman, PGA

Greens Fees

	9 Holes	18 Holes
Weekdays	$9.75	$15.75

Facilities/Services Available
Pro Shop • Putting Green •
Chipping Green • Snack Bar •
Dining Room • Dressing
Rooms (M & W) • Golf Lessons
• Group Play

Rental Equipment

	9 holes	18 holes
Carts	$10.50	$18.50
Pull Carts	$1.00	$1.00
Golf Clubs	$6.00	$6.00

Course Description –Three nine hole courses link up for what *Golf Magazine* rated among its "Best Bang for a Buck" listing. This is one of the busiest courses in the state, so a "Keep Pace" rule is encouraged. Challenge is heightened by water throughout.

1992 Champions –
Men's – Tony Johnson   Senior – Bud Humphreys
Women's – Lori Oldendick   Junior – Jon Sweeten

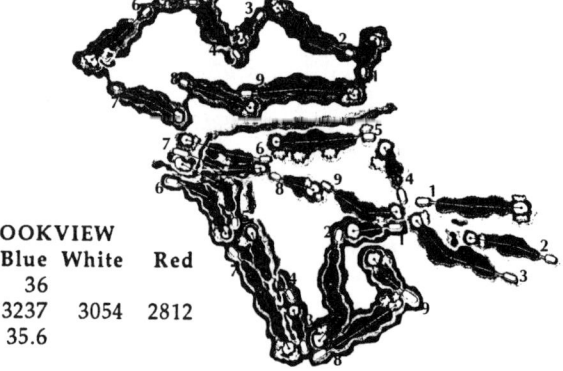

BROOKVIEW

Tees:	Blue	White	Red
PAR:	36		
Yardage:	3237	3054	2812
Rating:	35.6		

LAKEVIEW

Tees:	Blue	White	Red
PAR:	36		
Yardage:	3397	3169	2836
Rating:	36.5		

RIDGEVIEW

Tees:	Blue	White	Red
PAR:	34		
Yardage:	2713	2423	1913
Rating:	32.7		

Anderson/Lindsey Golf Course

7955 Wilson Road
Fort Knox, Kentucky
502-624-1548

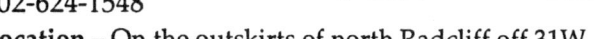

Location – On the outskirts of north Radcliff off 31W.

Private	Greens Fees Guests	
	Weekdays	$12.00
Year Round – 36 Holes	Evenings	$12.00
Pro – John W. "Tommy" Thompson, PGA	Weekends	$15.00

Facilities/Services Available
Pro Shop • Driving Range •
Putting Green • Chipping Green
• Snack Bar • Dining Room •
Lounge • Meeting Room •
Dressing Rooms (M & W) •
Showers (M) • Private Lockers
(M) • Golf Lessons • Club Repair
• Group Play • Memberships

Rental Equipment

	9 holes	18 holes
Carts	$7.00	$14.00
Pull Carts	$2.00	$2.00
Golf Clubs	$4.00	$4.00

Course Description –Both 18-hole courses feature tree-lined, narrow fairways. Greens are well-bunkered. Anderson is hilly and includes two water hazards. There is no water on the somewhat flatter Lindsey.

1992 Champions

Men's – Bill Jones

Women's – Joan Waldrop

Senior – Les McMannes
            Joe Harper
Junior – B. Irish

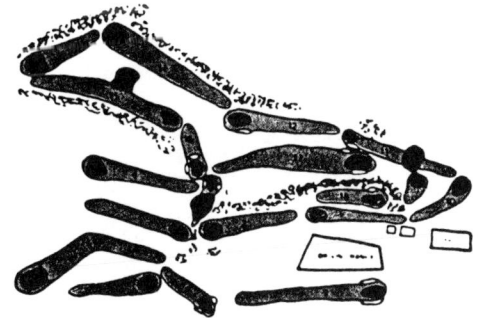

ANDERSON				LINDSEY			
Tees:	Blue	White	Red	Tees:	Blue	White	Red
PAR:	72	72	72	PAR:	72	72	72
Yardage:	6528	6274	5302	Yardage:	6661	6431	5302
Rating:	70.6	69.4	69.5	Rating:	70.6	69.4	69.5
Slope Rating:	116	114	113	Slope Rating:	116	114	113

Ft. Mitchell Country Club
250 Ft. Mitchell Avenue
Ft. Mitchell, Kentucky
606-331-4580

Location – Off Route 25 in Ft. Mitchell.

Private	**Greens Fees** Guests
March thru December – 9 Holes	Weekdays $20.00
Pro – Jack Merz, PGA	Weekends $25.00

Facilities/Services Available
Pro Shop • Driving Range •
Putting Green • Snack Bar •
Dining Room • Lounge •
Meeting Room • Dressing
Rooms (M & W) • Showers (M
& W) • Private Lockers (M &
W) • Golf Lessons • Club
Repair

Rental Equipment

	9 holes	18 holes
Carts	$10.50	$19.00
Pull Carts	$1.00	$2.00

Course Description – A bold design is punctuated with lots of
bunkers and tight, tree-lined fairways. Hills and valleys
prevail. Water enters play on only one hole.

1992 Champions –
Men's – Lee Davis
Women's – Cynthia Rorer

Tees:	White	Red
PAR:	35	37
Yardage:	2978	2725
Rating:	70.1	71.3
Slope Rating:	124	120

Highland Country Club
931 Alexandria Pike
Fort Thomas, Kentucky
606-441-8810

Location – Off 471 (Rt. 27 exit), 3-4 miles south of downtown.

Private
Year Round – 18 Holes
Pro – Jay Lumpkin, PGA

Greens Fees Guests
Weekdays $20.00
Weekends $25.00

Facilities/Services Available
Pro Shop • Putting Green •
Chipping Green • Practice
Bunker • Snack Bar • Dining
Room • Lounge • Meeting
Room • Dressing Rooms (M &
W) • Showers (M & W)) • Private
Lockers (M & W) • Golf Lessons
• Club Repair • Group Play •
Memberships

Rental Equipment
                      18 holes
Carts $20.00

Course Description – The Arthur Hills design is very hilly, with most tees and greens elevated against slim, tree-filled fairways. Sand is everywhere, and water creates perils on seven holes.

1992 Champions –
Men's – Randy Fritche   Senior – Jack Thelen
Women's – Ann Pawsat

Tees:	Blue	White	Red
PAR:	70	70	70
Yardage:	6280	5818	4799
Rating:	70.2	68.1	65.9
Slope Rating:	124	120	103

Frankfort Country Club

Two Creeks-County Lane Court
Frankfort, Kentucky
502-695-1403

Location – Two miles east of I-64 off U. S. 60.

Private
Year Round – 18 Holes
Pro – David S. Graf, PGA

Greens Fees Guests
Weekdays $20.00
Weekends $30.00

Facilities/Services Available
Pro Shop • Driving Range •
Putting Green • Chipping
Green • Snack Bar • Dining
Room • Lounge • Meeting
Room • Dressing Rooms (M &
W) • Showers (M & W) •
Private Lockers (M & W) •
Golf Lessons • Club Repair •
Group Play • Memberships

Rental Equipment

	9 holes	18 holes
Carts	$4.50	$9.00
Golf Clubs	$10.00	$15.00

Course Description – Formidable hazards are present on
nearly every hole of this scenic course. Parallel holes, 11 and
12, are separated by a lake. Water is also a major obstacle on
2 and 6. Bunkers dot each hole, and trees abound throughout.

1992 Champions –
Men's – Bruce Clark
Women's – Joan Harrod

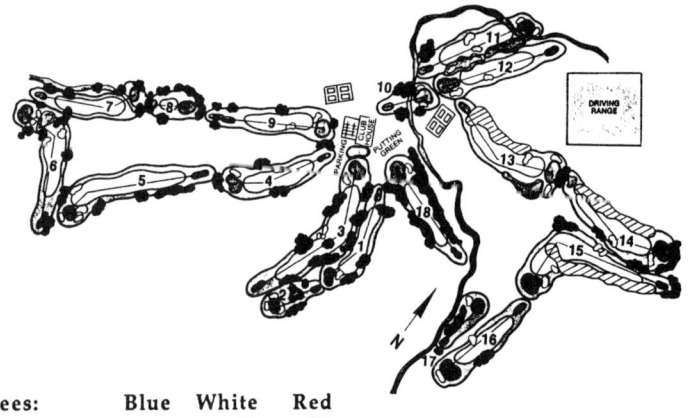

Tees:	Blue	White	Red
PAR:	72	72	72
Yardage:	6486	6095	5669
Rating:	70.5	68.7	71.7
Slope Rating:	125	121	124

Juniper Hills Golf Course
800 Louisville Road
Frankfort, Kentucky
502-875-8559

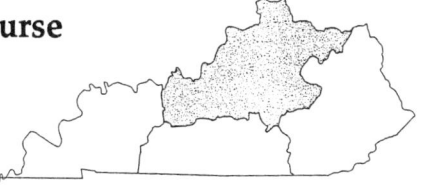

Location – Two miles east of I-64 on Highway 27.

Public

Year Round – 18 Holes

Golf Pro – Gene Hilen, PGA

Greens Fees
Weekdays $10.00
Evenings $6.00
Weekends $10.00
Season passes are available.
American Lung Association
Cards accepted.

Facilities/Services Available
Pro Shop • Putting Green •
Chipping Green • Practice
Bunker • Snack Bar • Meeting
Room • Dressing Rooms (M &
W) • Private Lockers (M & W) •
Golf Lessons • Club Repair •
Group Play • Season Tickets

Rental Equipment

	9 holes	18 holes
Carts	$9.00	$18.00
Pull Carts	$1.00	$2.00
Golf Clubs	$5.00	$10.00

Course Description – Buck Blankenship designed this course which tops tree-lined fairways with elevated small greens. A hilly landscape includes only one water hazard. A round can be played in 3-1/2 hours.

1992 Champions –
Men's – Chad Dawson   Senior – Jim Thompson
Women's – Ann French-Thomas

Tees:	Blue	White	Red
PAR:	70	70	74
Yardage:	6147	5954	5834
Rating:	67.5	65.6	70.5
Slope Rating:	104	102	106

Longview Country Club
3243 Frankfort Pike
Georgetown, Kentucky
502-863-6165

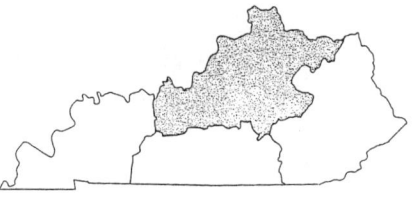

Location – Six miles west of Georgetown.

Semi-Private
Closed January – 18 Holes
Pro – Shawn Brookshire, PGA

Greens Fees Guests
Weekdays $9.00
Weekends $14.00

Facilities/Services Available
Pro Shop • Driving Range •
Putting Green • Chipping
Green • Snack Bar • Dining
Room • Lounge • Meeting
Room • Dressing Rooms (M &
W) • Showers (M & W) •
Private Lockers (M & W) •
Golf Lessons • Club Repair •
Group Play • Memberships

Rental Equipment

	9 holes	18 holes
Carts	$4.50	$9.00

Course Description – The biggest threat to par here is water.
Large bodies cut through 13, 14, 17 and line the green on 4.
Otherwise, fairways and greens are generous. Speed of play
rules are enforced.

1992 Champions –
Men's – Charles Kinney
Women's – Paula Bynum

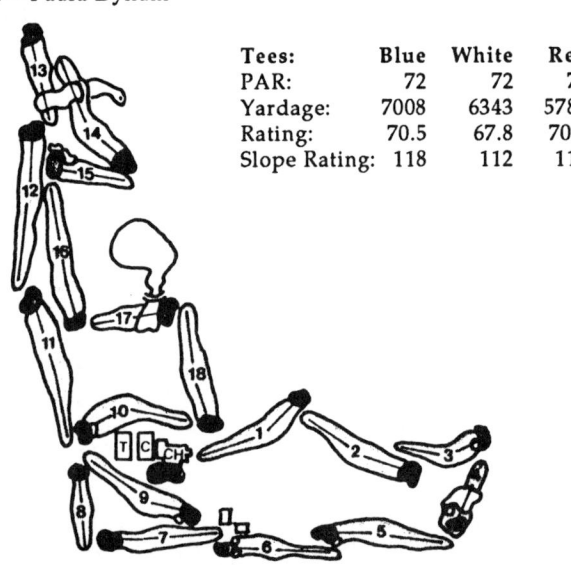

Tees:	Blue	White	Red
PAR:	72	72	75
Yardage:	7008	6343	5789
Rating:	70.5	67.8	70.2
Slope Rating:	118	112	116

Harmony Landing Country Club

Reading Road
Goshen, Kentucky
502-228-8316

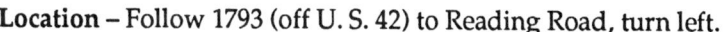

Location – Follow 1793 (off U. S. 42) to Reading Road, turn left.

Private
Year Round – 18 Holes
Pro – Mike Thomas, PGA

Greens Fees Guests
Weekdays $25.00
Weekends $35.00

Facilities/Services Available
Pro Shop • Driving Range • Putting Green • Chipping Green • Practice Bunker • Snack Bar • Dining Room • Meeting Room • Dressing Rooms (M & W) • Showers (M & W) • Private Lockers (M & W) • Golf Lessons • Club Repair • Memberships

Rental Equipment

	9 holes	18 holes
Carts	$10.00	$20.00
Golf Clubs	$10.00	$10.00

Course Description – Located in a suburb of Louisville, this course provides a rustic setting for a challenging round. Although the holes are well-guarded with bunkers and troubling trees, most paths are straight. Much of 18 is under water.

1992 Champions –
Men's – J. D. Conner   Senior – Bill Gibson
Women's – Louise Wilson

Tees:	Blue	White	Red
PAR:	71	71	74
Yardage:	6645	6392	5339
Rating:	71.7	70.4	70.3
Slope Rating:	127	124	120

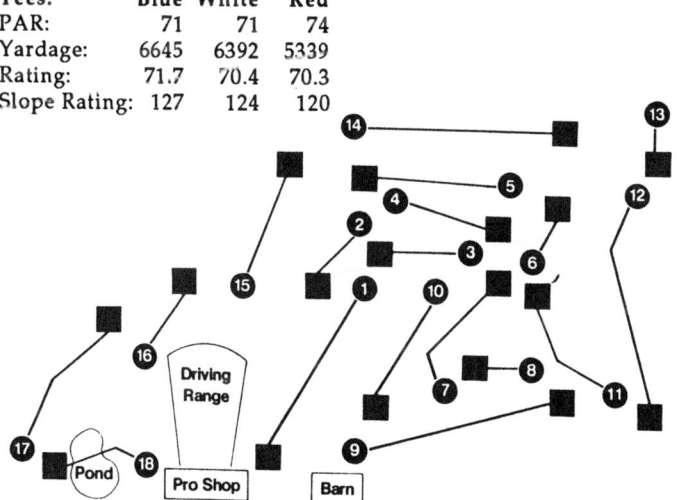

Breckinridge County Golf Center

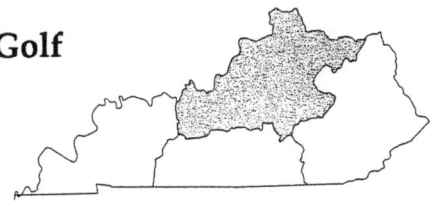

Highway 261 South
Hardinsburg, Kentucky
502-756-2842

Location – One-half mile north of Highway 60.

Semi-Private

Year Round – 9 Holes

Manager – Steve Puckett

Greens Fees

Weekdays	$7.00
Weekends	$15.00

Facilities/Services Available
Pro Shop • Driving Range •
Putting Green • Chipping
Green • Snack Bar • Meeting
Room • Private Lockers (M &
W) • Memberships

Rental Equipment

	9 holes	18 holes
Carts	$10.00	$15.00
Pull Carts		$5.00
Golf Clubs		$6.00

Course Description – Here is a 9-holer that's packed with punch. Although the hilly course is of medium length, the 606-yard no. 4 dogleg left is nothing to dismiss, nor is 7, a 519-yard dogleg right.

1992 Champions –
Men's – Robert Karman
Women's – Marian Robinson

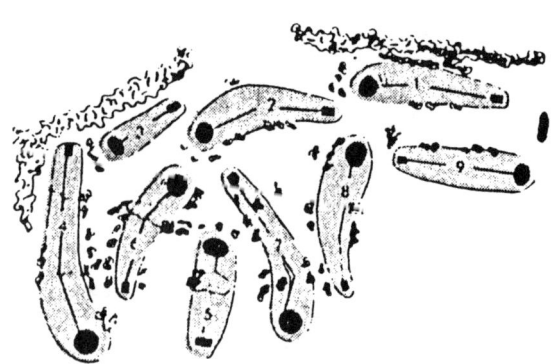

Tees:	Blue	White	Red
PAR:	36	36	36
Yardage:	3404	3312	2673
Rating:	71.5	70.7	69.5
Slope Rating:	118	116	112

Bright Leaf Golf Club
Danville Road
Harrodsburg, Kentucky
606-734-4231

Location – Two miles south of Harrodsburg on U. S. 27.

Semi-Private
Year Round – 27 Holes
Pro – Buck Blankenship, PGA

Greens Fees
Weekdays $14.00
Weekends $16.00

Facilities/Services Available
Pro Shop • Driving Range •
Chipping Green • Dining
Room • Lounge • Meeting
Room • Dressing Rooms (M &
W) • Golf Lessons • Club
Repair • Group Play •
Memberships

Rental Equipment

	9 holes	18 holes
Carts	$9.00	$18.00
Pull Carts	$2.00	$2.00
Golf Clubs	$5.00	$5.00

Course Description – Two regulation 18- and 9-hole courses make up this field. The 18-hole course is fairly open with five lakes that interfere with eight holes. Its 555-yard no. 7 includes a 200 yard carry over water and out of bounds on the left. A 9-hole par 3 is also part of the arena.

Tees:	18-Hole Blue	White	Red	Tees:	9-Hole Blue	White	Red
PAR:	72	72	77	PAR:	36	38	38
Yardage:	6615	5990	5411	Yardage:	3012	2626	2541
Rating:	69.7	68.5	65.4	Rating:			
Slope Rating:	117	114	118	Slope Rating:			

LaRue County Country Club
1175 Greensburg Road
Hodgenville, Kentucky
502-358-9727

Location – One mile south of Lincoln's birthplace on Highway 61.

Private **April thru October – 9 Holes**	**Greens Fees** Weekdays $6.00 Weekends $10.00

Facilities/Services Available
   Pro Shop • Putting Green •
   Snack Bar •Dressing Rooms (M
   & W) • Showers (M & W)   •
   Group Play • Memberships

Rental Equipment

	9 holes	18 holes
Carts	$7.00	$13.00

Course Description – This hilly course, located near the historic site of Lincoln's birthplace, has small, elevated greens.

Tees:	Blue	White	Red
PAR:	35	35	35
Yardage:	3135	3020	2910
Rating:	67.2	66.5	65.3
Slope Rating:	95	93	93

The Golf Courses at Kenton County

3908 Richardson Road
Independence, Kentucky
606-271-3200

Location – Four miles east of I-75 at Florence-Union exit, north to Industrial Road, right to Turkeyfoot, right to Richardson Road, turn left.

Public
Year Round – 54 Holes
Pro – Bill Gibbons, PGA

Greens Fees	9 Holes	18 Holes
Weekdays	$9 – $18	$12 – $30

Facilities/Services Available
Pro Shop • Driving Range • Putting Green • Chipping Green • Practice Bunker • Snack Bar • Meeting Room • Dressing Rooms • Showers • Private Lockers • Golf Lessons • Club Repair • Group Play •

Rental Equipment

	9 holes	18 holes
Carts	$10.00	$18.00
Pull Carts	$1.00	$1.00
Golf Clubs	$10.00	$10.00

Course Description – Three 18-hole Championship courses make up this 54 hole golf complex. Bent grass tees, greens, and fairways, highlight this challenging Arthur Hills design. Rated most difficult public course in Kentucky.

1992 Champions –
Men's – Greg Rice   Senior – Joe Leist
Women's – Barb Blank

FOX RUN

Tees:	Black	Blue	White	Red
PAR:	72	72	72	72
Yardage:	7055	6627	6107	4707
Rating:	74.8	72.9	70.5	64.1
Slope Rating	143	139	135	122

WILLOWS

Tees:	Blue	White	Red
PAR:	72	72	72
Yardage:	6791	6436	5669
Rating:	72.5	71.5	68.9
Slope Rating:	130	128	123

PIONEER

Tees:	Blue	White	Red
PAR:	70	70	71
Yardage:	6059	5759	5336
Rating:	67.9	67.3	65.0
Slope Rating	114	113	108

Estill County Golf Course
Old Pike
Irvine, Kentucky
606-723-5166

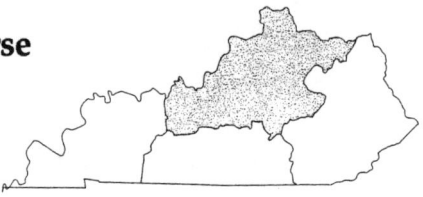

Location – One mile southeast of Irvine on Highway 1645.

Private
April thru October – 9 Holes
Club President – Phillip Dawes

Greens Fees
Weekdays $8.00
Weekends $10.00

Facilities/Services Available
   Pro Shop • Driving Range •
   Putting Green • Practice Bunker •
   Snack Bar • Lounge • Dressing
   Rooms (M & W) • Showers (M & W)
   • Private Lockers (M & W) •
   Group Play • Memberships

Course Description – Some water hazards increase difficulty
to an otherwise flat, easy to walk and enjoyable-to-play
course. Sand traps and bunkers.

1992 Champions –
Men's – Phillip Dawes   Senior – Freddie Withers
Women's – Patty Abney

Tees:	Blue	White	Red
PAR:	70	70	74
Yardage:	3103	2920	2551
Rating:	65.2		66.4
Slope Rating:	94		98

Oldham County Country Club

2300 N. Highway 393
LaGrange, Kentucky
502-222-9133

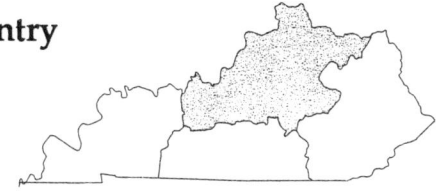

Location – Three miles north of I-71.

Semi-Private
Year Round – 18 Holes
Pro – Dave Van Meter, PGA

Greens Fees
Weekdays $12.00
Weekends $15.00

Facilities/Services Available
Pro Shop • Putting Green •
Snack Bar • Golf Lessons •
Club Repair

Rental Equipment

	9 holes	18 holes
Carts	$9.00	$16.00
Pull Carts	$2.00	$2.00
Golf Clubs	$10.00	$10.00

Course Description – Greens are armed with bunkers, while a creek meanders through several holes. A pond dips into 7. Most holes on this Buck Blankenship design are straight, with lengths of 145 to 523 yards.

1992 Champions –
Men's – Mark M. McDaniel   Senior – Jim Adams
Women's – Jenny Harsh

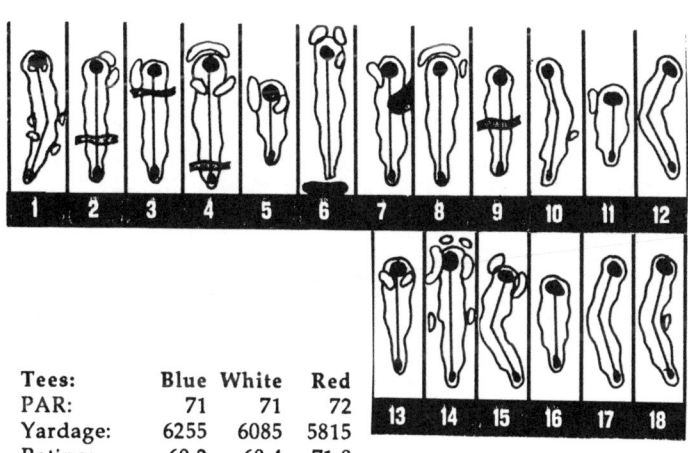

Tees:	Blue	White	Red
PAR:	71	71	72
Yardage:	6255	6085	5815
Rating:	69.2	68.4	71.8
Slope Rating:	115	113	118

Bob-O-Link Golf Course

Highway 62
Lawrenceburg, Kentucky
502-839-4029

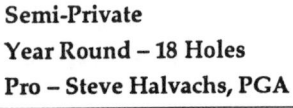

Location – One mile west of Highway 127.

Semi-Private
Year Round – 18 Holes
Pro – Steve Halvachs, PGA

Greens Fees
Weekdays $12.00
Weekends $15.00

Facilities/Services Available
Pro Shop • Driving Range •
Putting Green • Chipping
Green • Snack Bar • Dining
Room • Lounge • Meeting
Room • Dressing Rooms (M &
W) • Showers (M & W) •
Private Lockers (M) • Golf
Lessons • Club Repair •
Group Play • Memberships

Rental Equipment

	9 holes	18 holes
Carts	$10.00	$17.00
Pull Carts	$1.00	$2.00
Golf Clubs	$2.00	$4.00

Course Description – This rolling terrain features small greens and nine water hazards. A pond covers most of 8 and water is a major impediment on 10, 11 and 18. Eleven holes range under 400 yards.

1992 Champions –
Men's – Paul Goodlett
Women's – Laura Gillis

Tees:	Blue	White	Red
PAR:	71	71	71
Yardage:	6430	5925	4889
Rating:	70.4	70.4	70.4
Slope Rating:	109	108	105

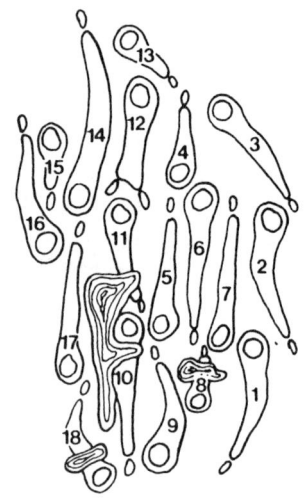

Knob View Golf Course

Preston Highway
Lebanon Junction, Kentucky
502-833-2253

Location – Exit 105 off I-65, 1/2 mile north on 61 (Preston Highway).

Public
March thru October – 9 Holes
Clubhouse Mgr – Margaret Ross

Greens Fees
Weekdays – $6.00
Weekends – $7.00
Pass programs available.
American Lung Association
Card accepted on weekdays.

Facilities/Services Available
Pro Shop • Putting Green •
Snack Bar • Group Play

Rental Equipment

	9 holes	18 holes
Carts	$8.00	$13.00
Pull Carts	$1.00	$1.00
Golf Clubs	$3.00	$3.00

Course Description – Tight, tree-lined fairways characterize this course. Three holes, 2, 3, and 8, are mounded.

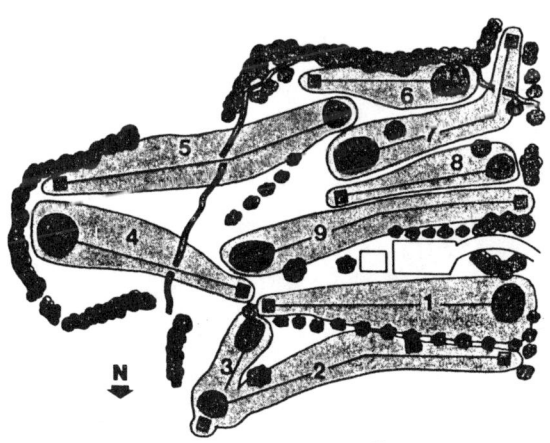

Tees:	Blue	White	Red
PAR:	36		38
Yardage:	2906		2906
Rating:	69		69

Lakeview Golf Course
Anneta Road on Route 259
Leitchfield, Kentucky
502-242-9971

Location – Five miles south of Western Parkway on 259.

	Greens Fees	
Private	Weekday	$8.00
Year Round – 9 Holes	Weekends	$10.00
Manager – Calvin Fulkerson		

Facilities/Services Available
Pro Shop • Driving Range •
Putting Green • Dining Room
• Meeting Room • Dressing
Rooms (M) • Showers (M) •
Private Lockers (M) • Group
Play • Memberships

Rental Equipment

	9 holes	18 holes
Carts	$8.00	$16.00
Pull Carts	$1.00	$1.00
Golf Clubs	$6.00	$6.00

Course Description – A long par 36 course includes several formidable problem areas. Between the tee and green on 7 is nothing but water. Lateral lake hazards complicate 4, 6 and 9.

1992 Champions –
Men's – Barry Alexander

Tees:	Blue	White	Red
PAR:	36	35	36
Yardage:	3420	3204	2604

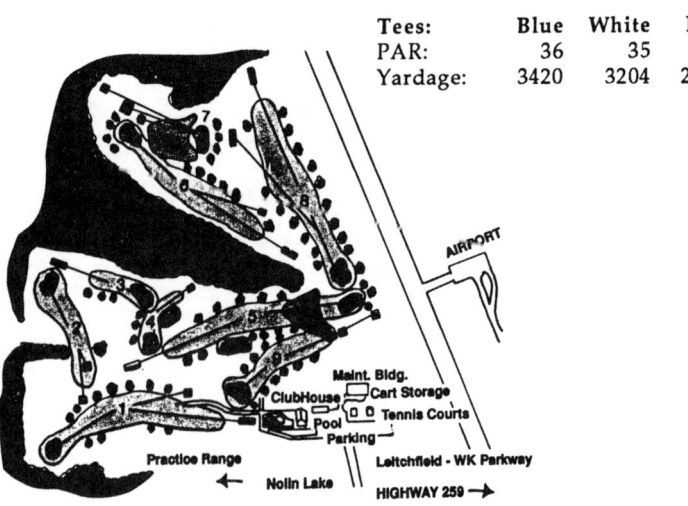

Andover Golf & Country Club

3450 Todds Road
Lexington, Kentucky
606-263-3710

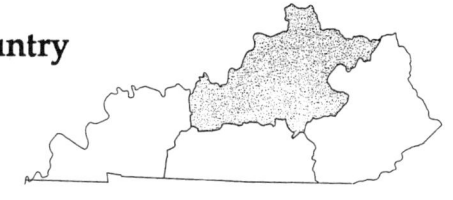

Location – One mile west of Man 'O War exit off I-75 on Todds Road.

Private
Year Round – 18 Holes
Pro – Danny McQueen, PGA

Greens Fees Guests
Weekdays $18.00
Weekends $23.00

Facilities/Services Available
Pro Shop • Driving Range •
Putting Green • Chipping
Green • Snack Bar • Dining
Room • Lounge • Meeting
Room • Showers •(M & W) •
Private Lockers (M & W) • Golf
Lessons • Club Repair • Group
Play • Memberships

Rental Equipment

	9 holes	18 holes
Carts	$10.00	$14.00
Pull Carts	$1.00	$2.00
Golf Clubs	$5.00	$10.00

Course Description – Here is an intriguing residential course. A short no. 2 involves shots over a lake to an ample green armed with Scottish style bunkers. On 16, a lake protrudes into play, and 18 has a bi-level fairway. Mounded throughout, trees and water also add to difficulty.

Tees:	Gold	Blue	White	Red
PAR:	72	72	72	72
Yardage:	6922	6519	6100	5249
Rating:	73.9	72.0	70.1	66.3
Slope Rating:	134	130	126	118

Campbell House Country Club

427 Parkway Drive
Lexington, Kentucky
606-254-3631

Location – Corner of South Broadway and Mason Headley.

Semi-Private

Year Round – 18 Holes

Pro – Chris Walton, PGA

Greens Fees
Weekdays $25.00*
Weekends $30.00*
*Includes cart.

Facilities/Services Available
Pro Shop • Putting Green •
Snack Bar • Dining Room •
Lounge • Meeting Room •
Dressing Rooms (M & W) •
Showers (M & W) •Private
Lockers (M & W) • Golf
Lessons • Club Repair •
Group Play • Memberships

Rental Equipment

	9 holes	18 holes
Pull Carts	$1.00	$2.00
Golf Clubs	$10.00	$10.00

Course Description – Formerly the Big Elm Country Club, a creek runs through this course, which has lateral water hazards on every hole. Quarries of varying sizes constitute other danger points on six holes.

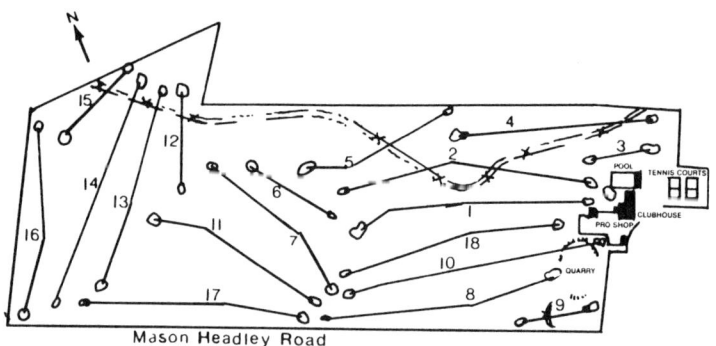

Tees:	Blue	White	Red
PAR:	70	70	74
Yardage:	6091	5940	5214
Rating:	69.4	68.8	70.0
Slope Rating:	117	116	116

Greenbrier Golf & Country Club

2179 Bahama Drive
Lexington, Kentucky
606-299-2811

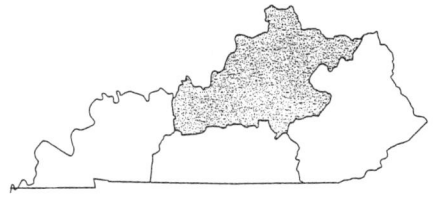

Location – Two miles east of I-75 on Winchester Road.

Private
March thru December– 18 Holes
Pro – Allan Freeman, PGA

Greens Fees Guests
Weekdays $35.00
Weekends $50.00

Facilities/Services Available
Pro Shop • Driving Range •
Putting Green • Chipping
Green • Dining Room •
Lounge • Meeting Room •
Dressing Rooms (M & W) •
Showers (M & W) • Private
Lockers (M & W) • Golf
Lessons • Memberships

Rental Equipment

	9 holes	18 holes
Carts	$9.00	$16.00
Golf Clubs	$10.00	$10.00

Course Description – The championship-caliber course has
nine water hazards which add the greatest challenge. Holes
3-8 are grouped around a lake that has finger creeks inter-
secting 3 and 12. Nos. 2, 6 and 11 are also major water holes.

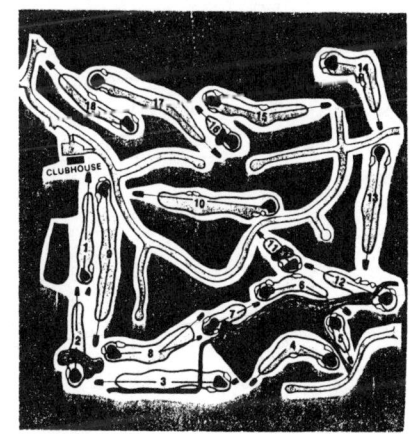

Tees:	18-Hole Blue	White	Red
PAR:	72	72	74
Yardage:	6754	6496	5592
Rating:	72.9	71.7	72.5
Slope Rating:	133	131	128

Idle Hour Country Club
1815 Richmond Road
Lexington, Kentucky
606-266-7901

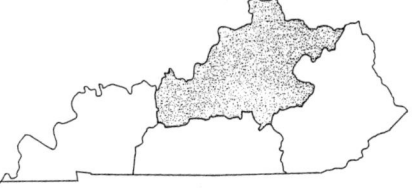

Location – One and one-half miles south of downtown Lexington.

Private
Year Round – 18 Holes
Pro – Gordon Leishman PGA

Greens Fees Guests
Weekdays $20.00
Weekends $30.00

Facilities/Services Available
Pro Shop • Driving Range •
Putting Green • Chipping
Green • Practice Bunker •
Snack Bar • Dining Room •
Lounge • Meeting Room •
Dressing Room (M & W) •
Showers (M & W) • Private
Lockers (M & W) • Golf
Lessons • Club Repair

Rental Equipment

	9 holes	18 holes
Carts	$8.00	$14.00

Course Description – This classic Donald Ross design includes narrow, well-bunkered fairways that are surrounded by mature trees. Three water hazards pose threats. Play is available only to members and their guests.

Tees:	Gold	Blue	White	Red
PAR:	71	71	71	73
Yardage:	6600	6387	6059	5097
Rating:	69.2	70.3	70.4	
Slope Rating:	132		130	122

Kearney Hill Golf Links
3403 Kearney Road
Lexington, Kentucky
606-253-1981

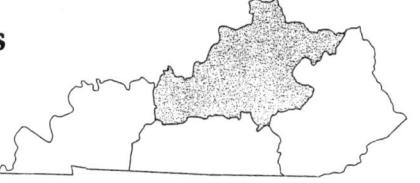

Location – Kentucky Horse Park exit off I-75, turn west onto Iron Works Pike; follow to Georgetown Road (Route 25), turn left, south two miles to Kearney Road, right one mile.

Public
Year Round – 18 Holes
Pro – Larry Smith, PGA

Greens Fees
Weekdays $20.00
Evenings $12.00*
Weekends $20.00
*After 5:00 P.M., May thru September.
Pass programs available.

Facilities/Services Available
Pro Shop • Driving Range • Putting Green • Chipping Green • Practice Bunker • Snack Bar • Meeting Room • Dressing Rooms (M & W) • Showers •(M & W) • Private Lockers (M) • Golf Lessons • Group Play

Rental Equipment

	9 holes	18 holes
Carts	$8.00	$16.00
Pull Carts	$3.00	$3.00
Golf Clubs	$12.00	$12.00

Course Description – A long, difficult and hilly course, greens and fairways are armed with both bunkers and water. No. 16 is likened to Pebble Beach's 18th, with water on the left, and trees on the right. Strategic accuracy is all that counts throughout. Home of Bank One Senior Golf Classic, Senior PGA Tour.

Tees:	Blue	White	Red
PAR:	72	72	72
Yardage:	6987	6501	5362
Rating:	73.5	70.5	70.1
Slope Rating:	128	122	118

Lakeside Golf Club

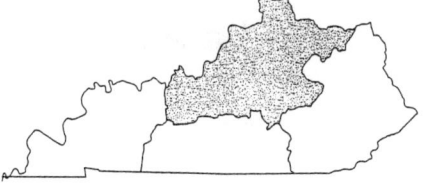

3725 Richmond Road
Lexington, Kentucky
606-263-5315

Location – Three miles from exit 104 on I-75, or 2 miles east from Circle 4.

Public

Year Round – 18 Holes

Pro – Al Chrouser, PGA

Greens Fees

Weekdays	$10.00
Evenings	$8.00
Weekends	$10.00

Seasonal Discount Card available.

Facilities/Services Available
Pro Shop • Driving Range •
Putting Green • Snack Bar •
Dressing Rooms (M & W) •
Golf Lessons • Club Repair •
Group Play

Rental Equipment

	9 holes	18 holes
Carts	$7.00	$14.00
Pull Carts		$3.00
Golf Clubs		$9.00

Course Description – 6844 yards of gently rolling golf. Central Kentucky's most played public golf course at over 65,000 rounds.

1992 Champions –
Men's – Rick Valentine
Women's – Sharron Park

Senior – Al Cummins
Junior – Guy Bradley

Tees:	Blue	White	Red
PAR:	72	72	72
Yardage:	6844	6521	5269
Rating:	72.2	70.9	69.8
Slope Rating:	123	120	116

Lexington Bluegrass Army Depot

Lexington Bluegrass Army Depot
Lexington, Kentucky
606-293-3600

Location – I-64 east to Haley Pike; follow Avon sign.

Semi-Private Year Round – 9 Holes

Greens Fees

Weekdays	$6.00
Evenings	$6.00
Weekends	$8.00

Facilities/Services Available
Pro Shop • Driving Range •
Putting Green • Snack Bar •
Dressing Rooms (M & W) •
Showers •(M & W) • Private
Lockers (M & W) • Member-
ships

Rental Equipment

	9 holes	18 holes
Carts	$6.00	$12.00
Pull Carts	$2.00	$2.00
Golf Clubs	$5.00	$5.00

Course Description – This course is laid out over rolling hills.
Two water hazards and twelve bunkers (with more planned)
increase the challenges. Small, fast greens, though, are what
make the course.

Tees:	Blue	White	Red
PAR:	36	36	36
Yardage:	3094	2964	2343
Slope Rating:	106	106	106

Lexington Country Club

5211 Paris Pike
Lexington, Kentucky
606-299-4388

Location – One mile west of I-75.

Private

Year Round – 18 Holes

Pro – Buddy Hartson, PGA

Greens Fees Guests
Weekdays $30.00
Weekends & Wednes. $35.00

Facilities/Services Available
   Pro Shop • Driving Range •
   Putting Green • Chipping
   Green • Practice Bunker •
   Snack Bar • Dining Room •
   Lounge • Meeting Room •
   Dressing Rooms (M & W) •
   Showers (M & W) • Private
   Lockers (M & W) • Golf Lessons
   • Club Repair • Memberships

Rental Equipment

	9 holes	18 holes
Carts	$10.00	$18.00
Pull Carts	$1.00	$2.00

Course Description – The slightly rolling terrain here is lined
with mature trees. Par 4s are very long, while putting
surfaces are large and fast. Pete Dye recently redesigned
one-third of the court.

1992 Champions –
Men's – Greg Engle   Senior – Mike Prunty
Women's – Dodgie Polites   Junior – Robbie Turner

Tees:	Blue	White	Red
PAR:	72	72	73
Yardage:	6994	6645	5692
Rating:	73.6	72.0	72.5
Slope Rating:	129	126	124

Marriott's Griffin Gate Resort

1720 Newtown Pike
Lexington, Kentucky
606-254-4101

Location – One-quarter mile south of I-64/75.

Resort
Year Round – 18 Holes
Director of Golf – Steve Hupe, PGA

Greens Fees

	Public/Guest-Member	
Weekdays	$44.00	$38.00
Weekends	$49.00	$38.00

Golf Cards accepted.

Facilities/Services Available
Pro Shop • Driving Net •
Putting Green • Chipping
Green • Snack Bar • Dining
Room • Lounge • Meeting
Room • Dressing Rooms (M &
W) • Showers •(M & W) •
Private Lockers (M & W) • Golf
Lessons • Club Repair • Group
Play • Memberships

Rental Equipment

	9 holes	18 holes
Carts (Included in Greens Fees)		
Golf Clubs	$8.00	$15.00

Course Description – This site of a Senior PGA Tour event for seven years was designed by Rees Jones, son of Robert Trent Jones. It has been rated among the top 75 resort courses in America by *Golf Digest*. Perils include eight water hazards and bunkers throughout.

Tees:	Gold	Blue	White	Red
PAR:	72	72	72	72
Yardage:	6801	6296	5948	4979
Rating:	73.3	71.5	69.5	
Slope Rating:	132	128	124	119

Players Club of Lexington

4850 Leestown
Lexington, Kentucky
606-255-1011

Location – 5.2 miles from New Circle Road, west of Lexington on Highway 421.

Semi-Private
Year Round – 18 Holes
Pro – Carmello Benassi, PGA

Greens Fees
Weekdays $25.00*
Evenings $20.00
Weekends $30.00*
*Includes cart.

Facilities/Services Available
  Pro Shop • Driving Range •
  Putting Green • Chipping
  Green • Practice Bunker •
  Snack Bar • Dining Room •
  Lounge • Dressing Rooms (W)
  • Showers (W) • Private
  Lockers (W) • Golf Lessons •
  Club Repair • Group Play •
  Memberships

Rental Equipment

	9 holes	18 holes
Pull Carts	$2.00	$3.00
Golf Clubs	$3.00	$5.00

Course Description – The first six holes are fairly straight and unthreatened. Water plays havoc on nos. 7, 8, 12, 14, 15 and 16. Several holes ramble more than 500 yards from the championship tees.

Tees:	Blue	White	Red
PAR:	72	72	72
Yardage:	6990	6385	5295
Rating:	72.0	73.2	68.7
Slope Rating:	128	116	121

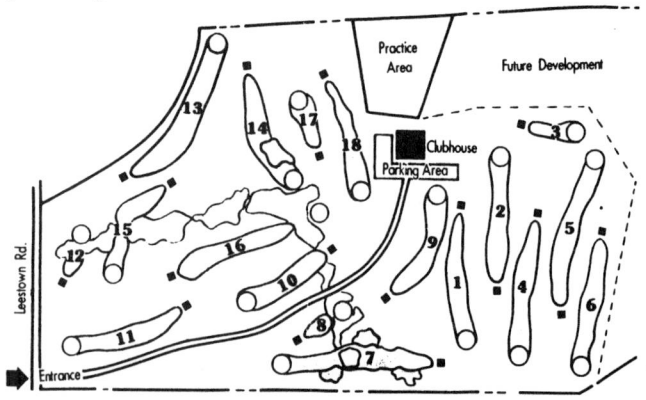

Spring Lake Country Club

Sandersville Road
Lexington, Kentucky
606-252-3854

Location – Ten minutes from I-75, off Georgetown Road.

Private
Year Round – 18 Holes
Pro – Stuart Beheler, PGA

Greens Fees Guests
Weekdays $20.00
Weekends $25.00

Facilities/Services Available
Pro Shop • Driving Range •
Putting Green • Chipping
Green • Practice Bunker •
Snack Bar • Dining Room •
Lounge • Meeting Room •
Dressing Rooms (M & W) •
Showers (M & W) • Private
Lockers (M & W) • Golf
Lessons • Club Repair •
Group Play • Memberships

Rental Equipment

	9 holes	18 holes
Carts	$7.10	$14.20
Pull Carts	$1.00	$1.00

Course Description – The front nine is fairly open, requiring long tee shots. The back nine has more character, with hilly terrain, three doglegs, two lakes, and a stream that serpentines through four holes.

Tees:	Blue	White	Red
PAR:	72	72	75
Yardage:	6948	5910	5568
Rating:	72.7	68.9	72.2
Slope Rating:	129	122	125

Tates Creek Golf Course
1400 Gainesway Drive
Lexington, Kentucky
606-272-3428

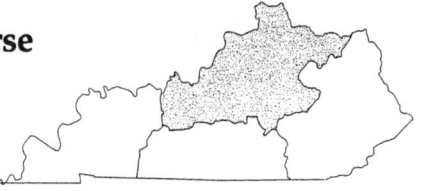

Location – First light south of New Circle Road on Tates Creek to Gainesway Drive.

Public
Year Round – 18 Holes
Golf Pro/Manager – Kim Murphy

Greens Fees
Weekdays $10.00
Evenings $8.00
Weekends $10.00
Pass programs available.

Facilities/Services Available
Pro Shop • Putting Green •
Chipping Green • Practice
Bunker • Snack Bar • Meeting
Room • Dressing Rooms (M &
W) • Showers (M) • Private
Lockers (M) • Golf Lessons •
Club Repair • Group Play

Rental Equipment

	9 holes	18 holes
Carts	$7.00	$14.00
Pull Carts	$3.00	$3.00
Golf Clubs	$9.00	$9.00

Course Description – The site of the Lexington City Championship is built on a rolling plane, which has tight, tree-lined fairways and three water hazards.

Tees:	Blue	White	Red
PAR:	72	7?	73
Yardage:	6240	5858	5260
Rating:	69.5	67.9	69.3
Slope Rating:	120	117	117

Audubon Country Club

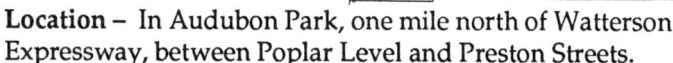

3265 Robin Road
Louisville, Kentucky
502-637-5625

Location – In Audubon Park, one mile north of Watterson
Expressway, between Poplar Level and Preston Streets.

Private
Year Round – 18 Holes
Pro – Dick Bradow, PGA

Greens Fees Guests
Weekdays $35.00
Weekends $35.00

Facilities/Services Available
Pro Shop • Driving Range • Putting
Green • Chipping Green • Practice
Bunker • Snack Bar • Dining Room
• Lounge • Meeting Room • Dress-
ing Rooms (M & W) • Showers (M &
W) • Private Lockers (M & W) • Golf
Lessons • Club Repair • Member-
ships

Course Description – Classic design features a great variety of
well-bunkered holes. Set on hilly terrain in an area known
for its beauty, many species of trees add to its appeal. All
major Kentucky golf championships have been held here.

1992 Champions –
Men's – Jim Ewald   Senior – Fred Allen
Women's – Susan Stewart   Junior – Terry Hyland
                                                      Laurie Gunderson

Tees:	Blue	White	Red
PAR:	72	72	74
Yardage:	6720	6386	5476
Rating:	73.3	71.8	72.4
Slope Rating:	135	132	128

Big Spring Country Club
Dutchmans Lane
Louisville, Kentucky
502-458-2027

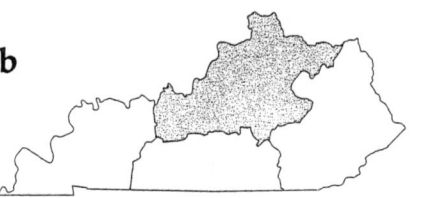

Location – One-half mile off I-64 and Cannons Lane.

Private
Year Round – 18 Holes
Pro – Lee Alexander, PGA

Greens Fees Guests
Weekdays – $35.00
Weekends – $50.00

Facilities/Services Available
Pro Shop • Driving Range •
Putting Green • Chipping
Green • Practice Bunker •
Snack Bar • Meeting Room •
Dressing Rooms (M & W) •
Showers •(M & W) • Private
Lockers • Golf Lessons •
Club Repair • Memerships

Rental Equipment

	9 holes	18 holes
Carts	$10.00	$18.00

Course Description – The site of the 1952 PGA Championship is armored with bunkers throughout. A creek creates three water hazards. Fairways are narrow and lined with matue trees.

1992 Champions –
Men's – Vince Hamilton
Women's – Joyce Brenzel

Senior – Ed Lowry Sr.
Junior – Jimmy Snider

Tees:	Blue	White	Red
PAR:	72	72	73
Yardage:	6657	6378	5593
Rating:	71.9	70.6	67.0
Slope Rating:	128	125	118

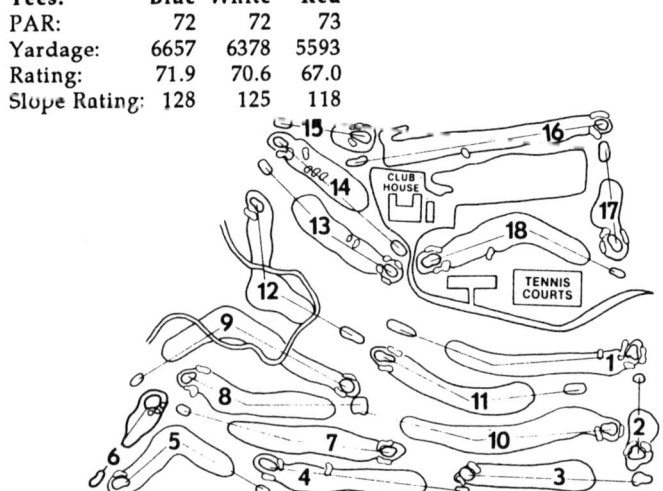

Bobby Nichols Golf Course

4301 East Pages Lane
Louisville, Kentucky
502-937-9051

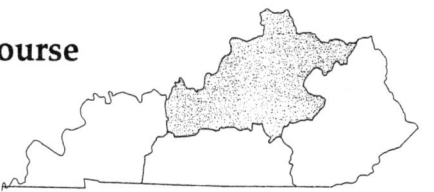

Location – One-half mile off Dixie Highway.

Public

Year Round – 9 Holes

Pro – Skip Welch, PGA

Greens Fees

Weekdays	$7.00
Evenings	$5.00*
Weekends	$8.00

*After 6:00 p.m.
Pass programs available.

Facilities/Services Available
Pro Shop • Driving Range •
Putting Green • Chipping
Green • Snack Bar • Dressing
Rooms (M & W) • Private
Lockers (M) • Golf Lessons •
Club Repair • Group Play

Rental Equipment

	9 holes	18 holes
Carts	$10.00	$18.00
Pull Carts	$2.00	$2.00
Golf Clubs	$5.00	$5.00

Course Description – Named for one of Louisville's most
successful golf prodigies, this versatile course provides
plenty of action. Two creeks wander through treed, hilly
landscape, creating a total of eight water hazards. Majority
of tightly-laid-out holes are par 4s and 5s.

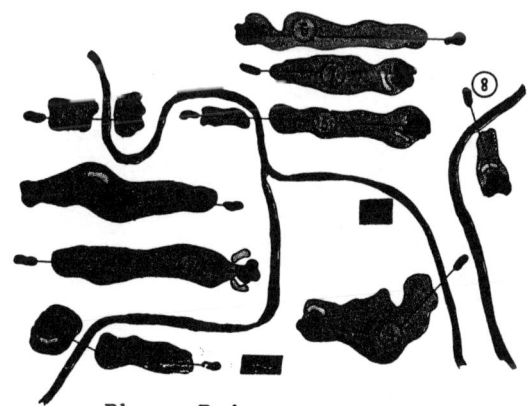

Tees:	Blue	Red
PAR:	36	37
Yardage:	3220	2818
Rating:	71.6	73.4
Slope Rating:	114	116

Charlie Vettiner Golf Course

10207 Mary Dell Lane
Louisville, Kentucky
502-267-9958

Location – Two miles north of Jeffersontown off Billtown Road.

Public
Year Round – 18 Holes
Pro – Carl Owen, PGA

Greens Fees

Weekdays	$6.00
Evenings	$6.00
Weekends	$6.00

Pass programs available.

Facilities/Services Available
Pro Shop • Putting Green •
Chipping Green • Snack Bar •
Dining Room • Dressing
Rooms (M & W) • Showers (M
& W) • Private Lockers (M & W)
• Golf Lessons • Club Repair
• Group Play

Rental Equipment

	9 holes	18 holes
Carts	$8.00	$16.00
Pull Carts	$1.00	$1.00
Golf Clubs	$4.00	$4.00

Course Description – A forked creek rambles through half of the holes. Lots of sand traps misplaced balls, while fairways give little leeway. Toughest test is on 9, a 538-yard par 5 that's cut in two by a stream.

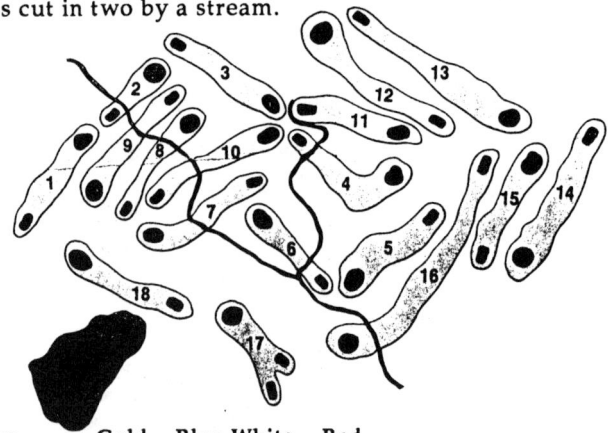

Tees:	Gold	Blue	White	Red
PAR:	72	72	72	75
Yardage:	6914	6507	6091	5388
Rating:	72.3	70.4	68.5	70.0
Slope Rating:	119		115	117

Cherokee Golf Course

Cherokee Parkway
Louisville, Kentucky
502-458-9450

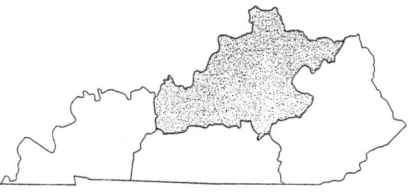

Location – Off Grinstead Drive exit off I-64.

Public
Year Round – 9 Holes
Pro – Mark Kemper, PGA

Greens Fees
Weekdays $6.00
Evenings $6.00
Weekends $6.00
Pass programs available.

Facilities/Services Available
Pro Shop • Driving Range •
Putting Green • Snack Bar •
Dressing Rooms (M & W) •
Golf Lessons • Club Repair •
Group Play

Rental Equipment

	9 holes	18 holes
Carts	$8.00	$14.00
Pull Carts	$1.50	$1.50

Course Description – A healthy workout for any golfer, this hilly course has ample-size fairways and greens. No. 6 requires a strong drive from the elevated men's tees over Cherokee Lake to approach dogleg left.

Tees:	Blue	White	Red
PAR:	36		36
Yardage:	2917	2778	2321
Rating:	66.8		66.8
Slope Rating:	103		101

Crescent Hill Golf Course
3110 Brownsboro Road
Louisville, Kentucky
502-896-9193

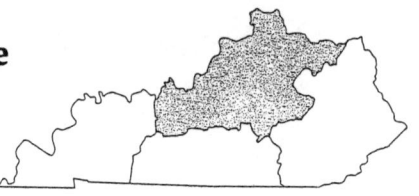

Location – East on U.S. 42 from Zorn Avenue exit off I-71.

Public
Year Round – 9 Holes
Pro – Doug Weick, PGA

Greens Fees
Weekdays $7.00
Evenings $5.00
Weekends $8.00
Pass programs available.

Facilities/Services Available
Pro Shop • Driving Range •
Putting Green • Snack Bar •
Dressing Rooms (M & W) •
Golf Lessons • Club Repair

Rental Equipment

	9 holes	18 holes
Carts	$10.00	$18.00
Pull Carts	$2.00	$2.00
Golf Clubs	$4.50	$4.50

Course Description – Links are hilly with groves of trees that complicate play throughout. Most rigorous layout is on the 476-yard no. 5, which has a mighty drop from the tees to a steep uphill dogleg right.

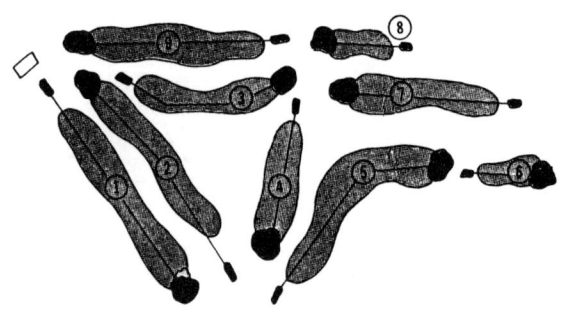

Tees:	Blue	White	Red
PAR:	36	36	38
Yardage:	3081	3007	2531
Rating:	68.0	67.3	67.3
Slope Rating:	104	103	103

Glen Oaks Country Club
10501 Old Brownsboro Road
Louisville, Kentucky
502-425-6100

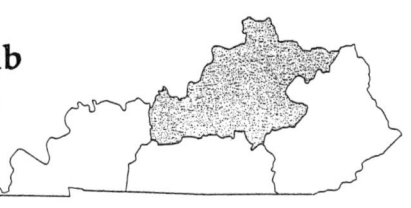

Location – Left on 1694 off I-71.

Private

18 Holes

Pro – Denny Thompson, PGA

Facilities/Services Available
Pro Shop • Driving Range • Putting
Green • Chipping Green • Practice
Bunker • Snack Bar • Dining Room •
Lounge • Meeting Room • Dressing
Rooms (M & W) • Showers (M & W) •
Private Lockers (M & W) • Golf
Lessons • Club Repair • Group Play
• Memberships

Course Description – New course, to open May 1993.

Tees:	Blue	White	Red	Yellow
PAR:	72	72	72	72
Yardage:	6770	6363	5292	5942

Glenmary Golf & Recreation Club

8501 Bardstown Road
Louisville, Kentucky
502-239-6601

Location – One mile south of Gene Snyder Freeway on Bardstown Road.

Semi-Private
Year Round – 18 Holes
Pro – Dennis Thompson, PGA

Greens Fees
Weekdays $17.00
Weekends $20.00

Facilities/Services Available
Pro Shop • Putting Green •
Snack Bar • Dining Room •
Lounge •Meeting Room •
Dressing Rooms (M & W) •
Showers (M & W) • Private
Lockers (M & W) • Golf
Lessons • Club Repair •
Group Play • Memberships

Rental Equipment

	9 holes	18 holes
Carts	$10.00	$19.00
Pull Carts	$2.00	$2.00

Course Description – This Florida-community style course, designed by John Addington, features golf holes bordered by homes and century-old trees. Fairways, stretched along forest ravines, overlook waterfalls and lakes. An historic home serves as the clubhouse.

Tees:	Blue	White	Red
PAR:	72	72	72
Yardage:	6645	6265	5705
Rating:	71.2	69.3	71.1
Slope Rating:	126	122	122

Hurstbourne Country Club
8222 Shelbyville Road
Louisville, Kentucky
502-425-0094

Location – Lyndon Lane off Shelbyville Road (U.S. 60).

Private
Year Round – 27 Holes
Pro – Jim Osborne, PGA

Facilities/Services Available
Pro Shop • Driving Range • Putting
Green • Chipping Green • Practice
Bunker • Snack Bar • Dining Room •
Lounge • Meeting Room • Dressing
Rooms (M & W) • Showers (M & W) •
Private Lockers (M & W) • Golf Lessons •
Club Repair • Memberships

Course Description – Originally built in 1966, Arthur Hills
redesigned this course in 1987. Slim fairways cut through
trees, and sand traps are scattered throughout. Six lakes and
a creek must be conquered. A 1913-yard par 3 course is also
part of this oustanding playing field.

1992 Champions –
Men's – Al Pipes   Senior – Dick Struck
Women's – Sherry Leavell   Junior – Jon Hoffman

Tees:	Gold	Blue	White	Red
PAR:	72	72	72	73
Yardage:	6886	6426	6064	5187
Rating:	72.8	70.7	69.1	69.5
Slope Rating:	130	126	123	120

Iroquois Golf Course
Southern Parkway
Louisville, Kentucky
502-363-9520

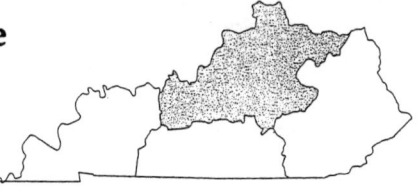

Location – Exit Southern Parkway off I-264.

Public **Year Round – 9 Holes** **Pro – Paul Schuchard, PGA**

Greens Fees
Weekdays $7.00
Weekends $8.00
Pass programs available.

Facilities/Services Available
Pro Shop • Driving Range •
Putting Green • Snack Bar •
Dressing Rooms (M & W) •
Showers (M & W) • Private
Lockers (M & W) • Golf
Lessons • Club Repair •
Group Play

Rental Equipment

	9 holes	18 holes
Carts	$10.00	$18.00
Pull Carts	$2.00	$2.00
Golf Clubs	$3.00	$3.00

Course Description – The front nine is wooded and moderately tight with tree-lined fairways. No water or sand interferes with play. Two holes are very long par 4s.

Tees:	Blue	Red
PAR:	71	74
Yardage:	6133	6049
Rating:	67.3	70.2
Slope Rating:	106	112

Louisville Country Club
6028 Upper River Road
Louisville, Kentucky
502-895-8477

Location – Follow U. S. 42 to Indian Hills Trail.

Private
Year Round – 18 Holes
Pro – Tommy Smith, PGA

Facilities/Services Available
 Pro Shop • Driving Range • Putting
 Green • Chipping Green • Practice
 Bunker • Snack Bar • Dining Room
 • Lounge • Meeting Room •
 Dressing Rooms (M & W) • Showers
 (M & W) • Private Lockers (M & W) •
 Golf Lessons • Club Repair

Course Description – The training ground for PGA Tour
champion Ted Schulz, rolling hills and woods are the setting
for this scenic challenge. Medium fairways and fast greens
are bolstered with sand.

Tees:	Blue	White	Red
PAR:	72	72	72
Yardage:	6512	6238	5340
Rating:	71.3	70.3	70.6
Slope Rating:	129	126	126

Oxmoor Golf & Steeplechase Course

9000 Limehouse Lane
Louisville, Kentucky
502-491-7877

Location – Lowe Road and Taylorsville Road on south section of Oxmoor Farm in east Louisville.

Private

Year Round – 18 Holes

Pro – Chris Brown, PGA

Greens Fees Guests

Weekdays	$25.00
Weekends	$35.00

Facilities/Services Available
Pro Shop • Driving Range • Putting Green • Snack Bar • Dining Room • Lounge • Meeting Room • Dressing Rooms (M & W) • Showers (M & W) • Private Lockers (M & W) • Golf Lessons • Club Repair • Group Play • Memberships

Rental Equipment

	9 holes	18 holes
Carts	$8.00	$16.00
Pull Carts	$2.00	$2.00

Course Description – Seven lakes, English-style berms, and dramatic placements of white sand bunkers and sculptured greens mark this David Pfaff design. The huge clubhouse overlooks the challenging, tree-filled golf arena and its unique, active steeplechase course.

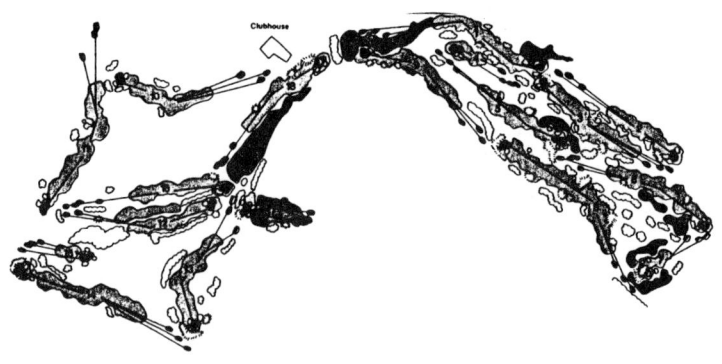

Tees:	Blue	White	Red
PAR:	72	72	74
Yardage:	6902	6489	5457
Rating:	72.0	70.9	71.2
Slope Rating:	128	125	122

Persimmon Ridge Golf Club

72 Persimmon Ridge Drive
Louisville, Kentucky
502-241-0819

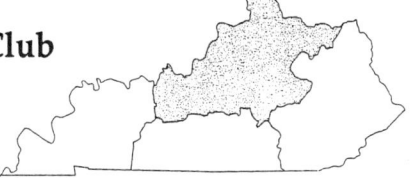

Location – Follow Long Run Road off U.S. 60, east of Louisville.

Semi-Private	
Year Round – 18 Holes	
Pro – Matt Taylor, PGA	

Greens Fees
Members/Non-Members
Weekdays $23.00/$39.50*
Weekends $29.00/$50.00*
*Includes cart.

Facilities/Services Available
Pro Shop • Driving Range •
Putting Green • Chipping Green
• Practice Bunker • Snack Bar
•Dining Room • Lounge •
Meeting Room • Dressing
Rooms (M & W) • Showers (M &
W) • Private Lockers (M & W) •
Golf Lessons • Club Repair •
Group Play • Memberships

Rental Equipment

	9 holes	18 holes
Carts	$5.00	$10.00
Golf Clubs	$8.00	$15.00

Course Description – Designed by noted architect, Arthur Hills, natural challenges await at every tee — from the split fairway on 3 to the waterlined fairway on 13. Practice area includes 23 acres. It was nominated to *Golf Digest* as "Best New Private Course in the Country" in 1990. Ranked nationally by *Golf Digest* and *Golf Week* in 1992.

1992 Champions –
Men's – Darrell Current   Senior – Fred Gupton
Women's – Susan Kirby-Spellman   Junior – Andy Just

Persimmon
Ridge

Tees:	Gold	Blue	White	Red
PAR:	72	72	72	72
Yardage:	7129	6593	6203	5284
Rating:	75.7	73.2	71.4	71.8
Slope Rating:	145	140	137	131

Polo Fields
1310 Flat Rock Road
Louisville, Kentucky
502-244-6688

Location – One mile north of U.S. 60 on Flat Rock Road.

Private
Year Round – 18 Holes
Pro – Tommie Mudd, PGA

Greens Fees Guests
Weekdays $22.00
Weekends $28.00

Facilities/Services Available
Pro Shop • Driving Range •
Putting Green • Golf Lessons •
Memberships

Rental Equipment
       18 holes
Carts $18.00

Course Description – New course, opens May 1, 1993. Challenging, bent grass tees, fairways, greens.

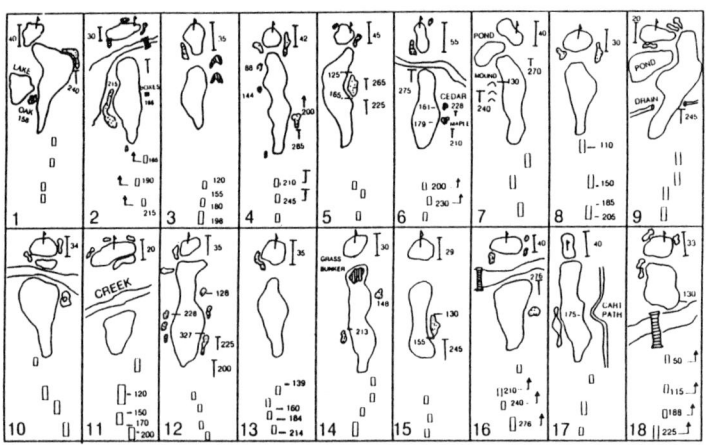

Tees:	Black	Blue	White	Red
PAR:	72	72	72	72
Yardage:	6965	6620	6147	5015

Quail Chase Golf Club

7000 Cooper Chapel Road
Louisville, Kentucky
502-239-2110

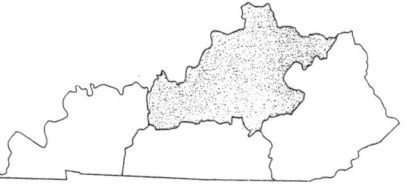

Location – Smyrna Road exit off Gene Snyder Freeway to Cooper Chapel Road at McNeely Lake.

	Greens Fees	
Public	Weekdays	$14.00
Year Round – 27 Holes	Evenings	$8.00
Pro – Shannon D. Shelton, PGA	Weekends	$16.00

Facilities/Services Available
Pro Shop • Driving Range •
Putting Green • Snack Bar •
Meeting Room • Dressing
Rooms (M & W) • Showers (M
& W) • Private Lockers (M & W)
• Golf Lessons • Club Repair
• Group Play • Memberships

Rental Equipment

	9 holes	18 holes
Pull Carts	$2.50	$2.50
Golf Clubs	$9.50	$9.50

Course Description – At last! A public course with country club standards. Quail Chase is your link to 27 holes of championship golf. *Golf Digest* rated Quail Chase as one of the premier courses to play. Rated as one of the best golf courses in the area by *Louisville Magazine*, 1991-1992.

Club Champions –
Men's – Matt Holmes
Women's – Marcia Alexander

Tees:	Gold	Blue	White	Red
PAR:	72	72	72	72
Yardage:	6786	6440	6061	5361
Rating:	71.9	70.4	68.7	65.5
Slope Rating:	124	121	118	111

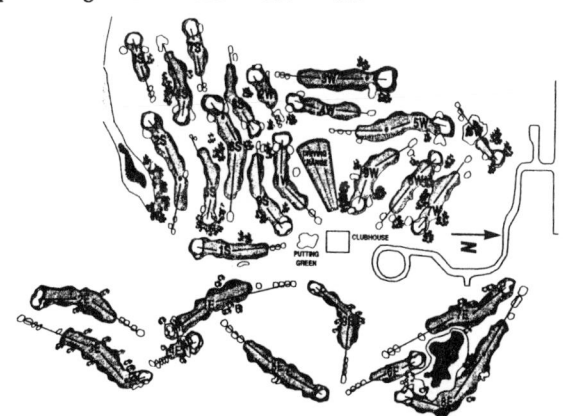

River Road Country Club

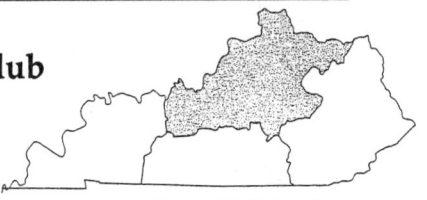

2930 Upper River Road
Louisville, Kentucky
502-893-2536

Location – At I-71 and Zorn Avenue across from Holiday Inn.

Private	
Year Round – 9 Holes	
Pro – Gene Swinney, PGA	

Greens Fees Guests
Weekdays $15.00
Weekends $25.00

Facilities/Services Available
Pro Shop • Driving Range •
Putting Green • Chipping Green
• Practice Bunker • Snack Bar •
Dining Room • Lounge • Meeting
Room • Dressing Rooms (M & W)
• Showers (M & W) • Private
Lockers (M & W) • Golf Lessons •
Club Repair • Group Play •
Memberships

Rental Equipment

	9 holes	18 holes
Carts	$10.00	$17.00
Pull Carts	$2.00	$3.00
Golf Clubs	$10.00	$10.00

Course Description – Set on the banks of the Ohio River, this is a difficult, flat course. Tight fairways are separated by trees. No. 4 is a treacherous 554-yard par 5. Trees near green on 8 threaten par, while the "Big Bertha" bunker on 9 will capture and imprison hooks.

1992 Champions –
Men's – Jim Greene   Junior – Seth Collins
Women's – Susan Cummins

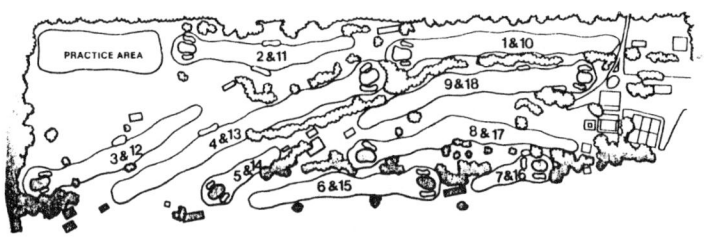

Tees:	Blue	White	Red
PAR:	36	36	38
Yardage:	3283	3376	3062
Rating:	71.4		74.7
Slope Rating:	125		129

Seneca Golf Course

2300 Seneca Park Road
Louisville, Kentucky
502-458-9298

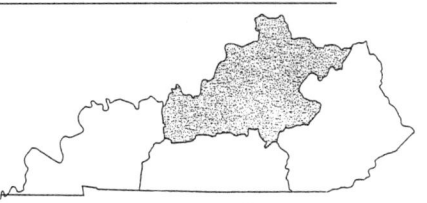

Location – Next to Bowman Field Airport, 1/2 mile from I-64.

Public
Year Round – 18 Holes
Pro – Eddie Tyree, PGA

Greens Fees

Weekdays	$7.00
Evenings	$5.00
Weekends	$8.00

Pass programs available.

Facilities/Services Available
Pro Shop • Driving Range •
Putting Green • Chipping
Green • Practice Bunker •
Snack Bar • Lounge • Meeting
Room • Dressing Rooms (M &
W) • Showers (W) • Private
Lockers (M & W) • Golf Lessons • Club Repair • Memberships

Rental Equipment

	9 holes	18 holes
Carts	$10.00	$18.00
Pull Carts	$3.00	$3.00
Golf Clubs	$5.00	$5.00

Course Description – Gary Player won his first PGA tournament here, the 1957 Derby Open. Against a rolling background, course includes two water holes. Groves of trees spark challenge as well.

1992 Champions –
Men's – Dan Utley   Senior – Evert Vaughan
Women's – Peg Escola   Junior – Danny Baron

Tees:	Blue	White	Red
PAR:	72	72	73
Yardage:	7010	6621	5821
Rating:	72.8	70.8	71.4
Slope Rating:	116	113	112

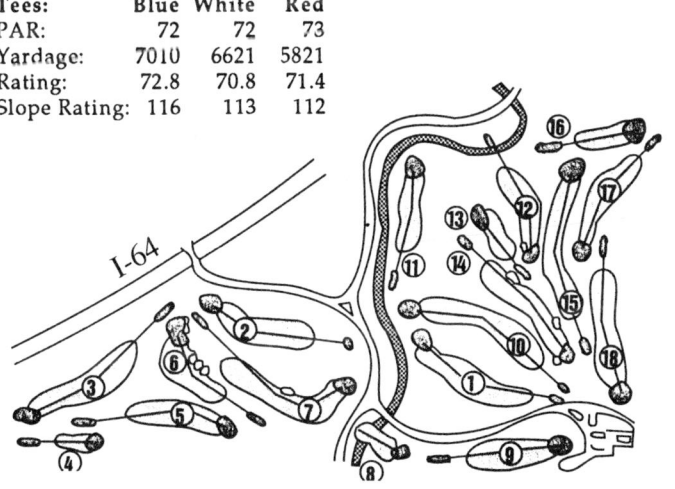

Shawnee Golf Course

460 Northwestern Parkway
Louisville, Kentucky
502-776-9389

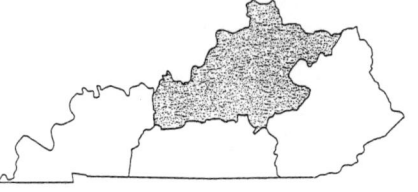

Location – Shively exit off I-64 to Northwestern Bank Street exit.

Public
Year Round – 18 Holes
Pro – Moe Demling, PGA

Greens Fees
Weekdays $6.00
Evenings $6.00
Weekends $6.00
Pass programs available.

Facilities/Services Available
Pro Shop • Driving Range •
Putting Green • Chipping
Green • Snack Bar • Meeting
Room • Dressing Rooms (M &
W) • Showers (M & W) •
Private Lockers (M & W) • Golf
Lessons • Club Repair •
Group Play

Rental Equipment

	9 holes	18 holes
Carts	$10.00	$18.00
Pull Carts	$3.00	$3.00

Course Description –PGA Tour champion Jodie Mudd got his start on this course. A flat layout runs along the Ohio River, it has recently undergone $.5 million renovation. The river is in view on 15-17. No. 2 may be the toughest par 4 in Louisville.

Tees:	Blue	White	Red
PAR:	69		69
Yardage:	6175	5923	5382

Standard Country Club

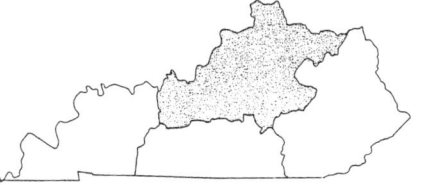

8208 Brownsboro Road
Louisville, Kentucky
502-425-1141

Location – Follow Old Brownsboro Road (U.S. 22) to Barbour Lane.

Private

Year Round – 18 Holes

Pro – Stacy Russell, PGA

Facilities/Services Available
  Pro Shop • Driving Range •
  Putting Green • Dining Room
  • Lounge • Meeting Room •
  Dressing Rooms (M & W) •
  Showers (M) • Private Lockers
  (M & W) • Golf Lessons • Club
  Repair • Group Play •
  Memberships

Rental Equipment

	9 holes	18 holes
Carts	$5.40	$10.60
Pull Carts	$1.25	$2.50

Course Description – A relatively flat course, these links have tree-lined fairways and gradually-sloping greens that are well protected by sand. One of the most challenging holes is no. 12, a 168-yard par 3 over water.

1992 Champions –
Men's – Gail Pohn
Women's – Bettie Watson

Junior – Josh Engel

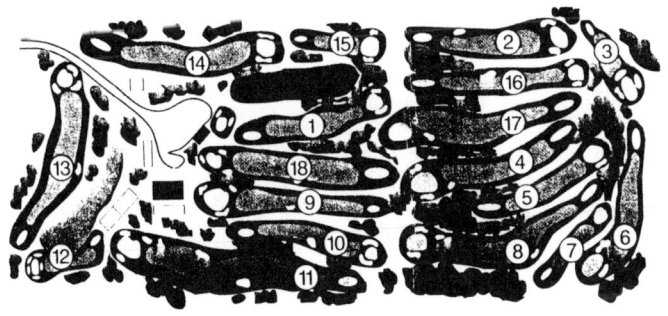

Tees:	Blue	White	Red	Senior
PAR:	72	72	76	72
Yardage:	6641	6495	6030	6110
Rating:	72.1	71.4	74.6	69.3
Slope Rating:	127	126	129	122

Valhalla Golf Club

15503 Shelbyville Road
Louisville, Kentucky
502-245-4475

Location – On U.S. 60, east of Louisville.

Private

Closed January – 18 Holes

Pro – Tony Pancake, PGA

Facilities/Services Available
Pro Shop • Driving Range • Putting
Green • Chipping Green • Practice
Bunker • Snack Bar • Dining Room •
Lounge • Dressing Rooms (M & W) •
Showers (M & W) • Private Lockers (M
& W) • Golf Lessons • Club Repair •
Memberships • Caddie Program

Course Description – This championship course, designed by
Jack Nicklaus, emphasizes quality and conditioning. A
finalist for *Golf Digest's* "Best New Private Clubs" in 1987, it
was also voted the top course in Kentucky by the magazine
in 1989 and 1991. The course record of 66 is held by Jack
Nicklaus, set at the grand opening in 1986. It is the site of
the 1996 PGA Championship.

Tees:	Gold	Blue	White	Red
PAR:	72	72	72	72
Yardage:	7087	6539	6104	5030
Rating:	73.9	71.0	68.8	68.6
Slope Rating:	133	127	122	118

Wildwood Country Club

5000 Bardstown Road
Louisville, Kentucky
502-499-1001

Location – Five miles south of I-264.

| Private |
| Year Round – 18 Holes |
| Pro – Gene Sullivan, PGA |

Greens Fees Guests
Weekdays $25.00
Weekends $30.00/$25.00

Facilities/Services Available
Pro Shop • Driving Range •
Putting Green • Chipping Green
• Practice Bunker • Snack Bar •
Dining Room • Lounge • Meeting Room • Dressing Rooms (M &
W) • Showers (M & W) • Private
Lockers (M & W) • Golf Lessons •
Club Repair • Group Play •
Memberships

Rental Equipment

	9 holes	18 holes
Carts	$8.00	$16.00
Pull Carts	$1.00	$1.00

Course Description – Golfers are rewarded more for accuracy
than for distance on this rolling, tight course. Versatility in
playing different lies is essential, as level lies are scarce or
nonexistent on some holes. The 18th hole is an appropriate
end to a challenging day.

1992 Champions –
Men's – Jim Hubbs
Women's – Joyce Denham

Tees:	Blue	White	Red
PAR:	72	72	75
Yardage:	6495	6320	6230
Rating:	70.1	69.1	70.6
Slope Rating:	121	119	120

Woodhaven Country Club

7200 Woodhaven Road
Louisville, Kentucky
502-491-9100

Location – Off Bardstown Road, south of Watterson Trail.

Private

Year Round – 18 Holes

Pro – Eddie Mudd, PGA

Greens Fees Guests
Weekdays $12.00
Weekends $20.00

Facilities/Services Available
Pro Shop • Driving Range •
Putting Green • Chipping
Green • Practice Bunker •
Snack Bar • Dining Room •
Lounge • Meeting Room •
Dressing Rooms (M & W) •
Showers (M & W) • Private
Lockers (M & W) • Golf Les-
sons • Club Repair • Group
Play • Memberships

Rental Equipment

	9 holes	18 holes
Carts	$10.00	$17.00
Pull Carts	$2.00	$3.00

Course Description – A serene but sneaky and tough course rambles through rolling farmland. Tree-lined fairways and small greens stiffen the demands, as do four water holes. A 9-hole par 3 is also attached.

1992 Champions –
Men's – Terry Hammann
Women's – Polly Ashby

Senior – Tim Conliffe
Junior – Derik Risk

Tees:	Blue	White	Red
PAR:	72	72	74
Yardage:	6590	6372	6230
Rating:	70.3	69.2	71.1
Slope Rating:	117	114	117

Kenton Station Golf Course
Route 2
Maysville, Kentucky
606-759-7154

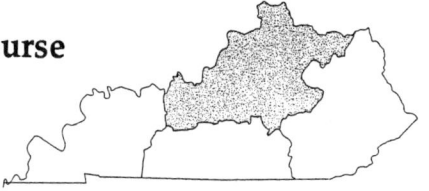

Location – One mile west of U.S. 68 on new A.A. Highway.

Semi-Private
Year Round – 9 Holes
Owner – Kearn McHugh

Greens Fees
Weekdays $6.00
Weekends $8.00

Facilities/Services Available
Pro Shop • Driving Range •
Putting Green • Snack Bar •
Lounge • Meeting Room •
Dressing Rooms (M & W) •
Showers (M & W) • Private
Lockers (M & W) • Golf Les-
sons • Club Repair • Group
Play • Memberships

Rental Equipment

	9 holes	18 holes
Carts	$3.00	$6.00
Pull Carts	$.50	$.75
Golf Clubs	$2.00	$3.00

Course Description – This straight, short course has its
aggravations. A large pond is shared by 6 and 8. Bunkers are
a test on most holes. The longest hole, no. 7, is a 420-yard
par 4 with a fair-sized green.

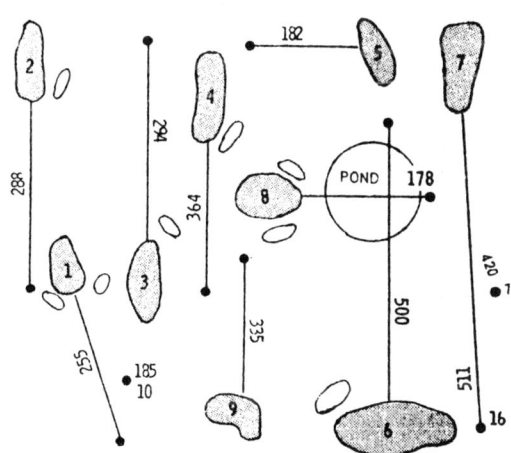

Tees:	Blue	White	Red
PAR:	35	35	36
Yardage:	2718	2816	2541

Maysville Country Club

1099 U.S. 68 South
Maysville, Kentucky
606-564-6351

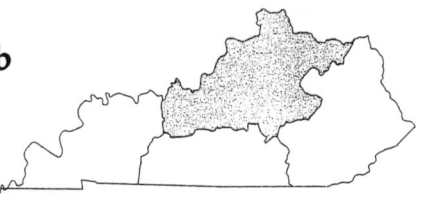

Location – Fifty miles east of Cincinnati on U. S. 68-S.

Semi-Private

March thru November – 18 Holes

Pro Shop Manager – Rita Blakefield

Greens Fees Guests

	w/members	w/non-members
Weekdays	$15.00/$25.00	
Weekends	$15.00/$25.00	

Facilities/Services Available
Pro Shop • Putting Green •
Chipping Green • Snack Bar •
Dining Room • Lounge •
Meeting Room • Dressing
Rooms (M & W) • Showers (M
& W) • Private Lockers (M &
W) • Golf Lessons • Club
Repair •Memberships

Rental Equipment

	9 holes	18 holes
Carts	$8.00	$15.00

Course Description – Level lies are difficult to achieve on this rolling course. Dense trees line holes, while three water hazards come into play.

1992 Champions –
Men's – Dave Grayson
Women's – Pauline Bierlin

Tees:	Gold	Blue	White	Red
PAR:	75	72	72	75
Yardage:	4658	6441	6048	5160
Rating:	65.3	70.5	68.2	68.8
Slope Rating:	105	118	113	112

Henry County Country Club
Highway 421
New Castle, Kentucky
502-845-2375

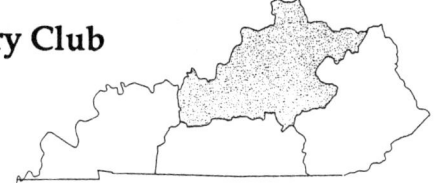

Location – I-71 exit 28, turn right; left on 146 for 9 miles to 421.

Semi-Private
Year Round – 18 Holes
Pro – Mike Phelps, PGA

Greens Fees

Weekdays	$9.00
Evenings	$6.00
Weekends	$12.00

Facilities/Services Available
Pro Shop • Driving Range •
Putting Green • Snack Bar •
Dressing Rooms (M & W) •
Showers (M & W) • Golf
Lessons • Club Repair •
Group Play • Memberships

Rental Equipment

	9 holes	18 holes
Carts	$6.00	$10.00
Pull Carts	$2.00	$2.00

Course Description – Sand, sand and more sand — 36 bunkers in all — stiffens the challenge here. A hilly terrain includes four lakes that enter play. Fairways are wide open and greens are fast.

Tees:	Blue	White	Red
PAR:	71	71	70
Yardage:	6525	6204	4660
Rating:	71.2	69.8	66.7
Slope Rating:	124	121	111

The Champions Golf Club

20 Avenue of Champions
Nicholasville, Kentucky
606-223-7272

Location – Six miles south of Lexington off Harrodsburg Road.

Private

Year Round – 18 Holes

Pro – Steve Smitha, PGA

Greens Fees Guests
Weekdays $37.00
Weekends $47.00

Facilities/Services Available
Pro Shop • Driving Range •
Putting Green • Chipping
Green • Practice Bunker •
Snack Bar • Dining Room •
Lounge • Meeting Room •
Dressing Rooms (M & W) •
Showers (M & W) • Private
Lockers (M & W) • Golf
Lessons • Club Repair •
Memberships

Rental Equipment

	9 holes	18 holes
Carts	$8.50	$17.00

Course Description – On this Arthur Hills design, ominous bunkers and trees abound. Water comes into play on seven holes. Fairways are extremely tight, and overall, the course lives up to its name.

1992 Champions –
Men's – Dwaine Ganding   Senior – Bob Nelson
Women's – Martha Humin   Junior – Jeremy Langley

Tees:	Gold	Blue	White	Red
PAR:	72	72	72	72
Yardage:	7081	6583	6109	5255
Rating:	74.7	72.5	70.4	71.1
Slope Rating:	137	133	129	120

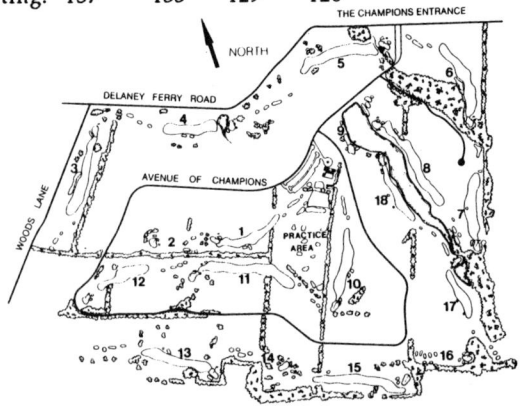

Connemara Golf Course
2327 Lexington Road
Nicholasville, Kentucky
606-885-4331

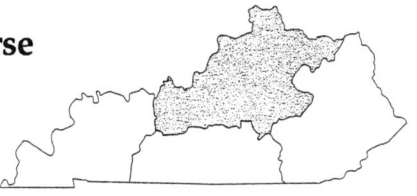

Location – Five miles south of Fayette Mall on Nicholasville Road.

Public
Year Round – 18 Holes
Pro – Bill Ridge, PGA

Greens Fees

	9 Holes	18 Holes
Weekdays	$10.00	$12.00
Weekends	$10.00	$19.50

Before 11:00 A.M. Weekdays – $16.95 (includes cart).

Facilities/Services Available
Pro Shop • Driving Range • Putting Green • Chipping Green • Practice Bunker • Snack Bar • Dressing Rooms (M & W) • Showers (M) • Private Lockers (M & W) • Golf Lessons • Club Repair • Group Play

Rental Equipment

	9 holes	18 holes
Carts	$5.00	$8.50

Course Description – Bent grass tees, greens and fairways. Old horse farm, 160 acre links type course. Original fences separate some fairways. Gently rolling fields.

Tees:	Blue	White	Red
PAR:	71	71	71
Yardage:	6533	6264	5000
Rating:	71.1	69.5	69.7
Slope Rating:	115	111	110

Lone Oak Country Club

Lone Oak Drive
Nicholasville, Kentucky
606-887-2212

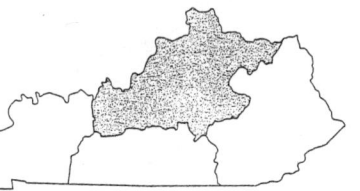

Location – One mile west of town on Kentucky 29.

Private	**Greens Fees** Guests
Year Round – 18 Holes	Weekdays $12.00
Secretary – Pam Burdine	Weekends & Holidays $22.00

Facilities/Services Available
Pro Shop • Driving Range •
Putting Green • Snack Bar •
Dining Room • Lounge •
Showers (M) •Private Lockers
(M & W) • Club Repair

Rental Equipment

	9 holes	18 holes
Carts	$8.00	$16.00
Pull Carts	$1.50	$2.00

Course Description – The prominent feature on this course is three lakes that must be crossed five times. Plenty of sand also increases degree of difficulty.

1992 Champions –
Men's – Tim Spivey
Women's – Marsha Boardus

Tees:	Blue	White	Red
PAR:	71	71	76
Yardage:	6473	6182	5506
Rating:	69.8	68.5	70.7
Slope Rating:	119	116	118

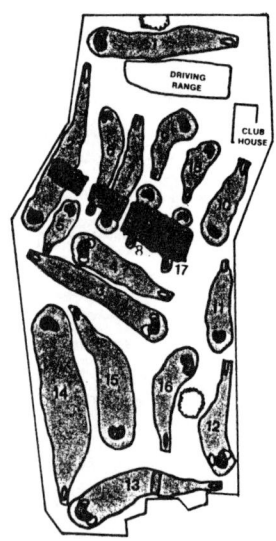

Shady Brook Golf Club
444 Hutchinson Road
Paris, Kentucky
606-987-1544

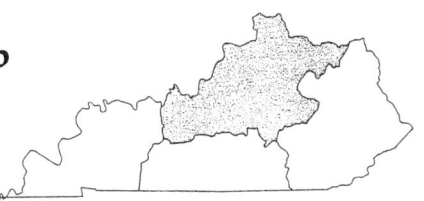

Location – On KY 1939, one mile east of U.S. 27.

KGA – Public	
Year Round – 9 Holes	
Pro – Bill Nash, PGA	

Greens Fees

Weekdays	$7.50
Weekends	$8.50

Facilities/Services Available
Pro Shop • Putting Green •
Snack Bar • Golf Lessons •
Club Repair • Group Play

Rental Equipment

	9 holes	18 holes
Carts	$8.00	$16.00
Pull Carts	$1.00	$1.50
Golf Clubs	$3.50	$5.00

Course Description – Located in the heart of central Kentucky's horse country, this course is challenged most by four water hazards. Trees are abundant throughout the scenic layout.

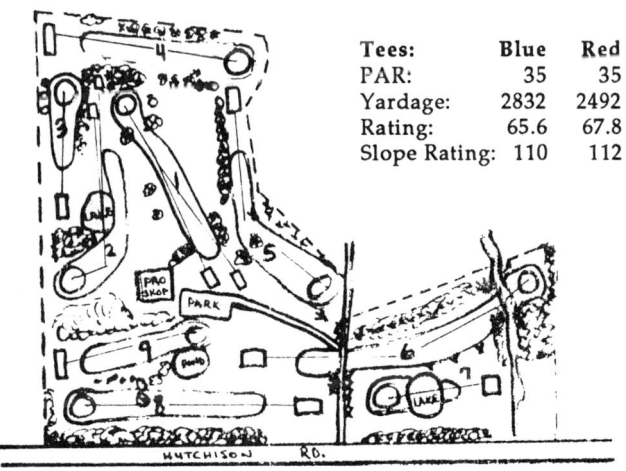

Tees:	Blue	Red
PAR:	35	35
Yardage:	2832	2492
Rating:	65.6	67.8
Slope Rating:	110	112

Hunting Creek Country Club
Highway 42
Prospect, Kentucky
502-228-8129

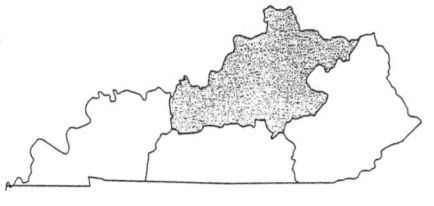

Location – Seven miles east of Watterson Expressway on Highway 42.

Private	
Year Round – 18 Holes	
Golf Pro – John McGuire, PGA	

Greens Fees Guests
Weekdays $25.00
Weekends $25.00

Facilities/Services Available
Pro Shop • Driving Range •
Putting Green • Snack Bar •
Dining Room • Lounge •
Meeting Room • Dressing
Rooms (M & W) • Showers (M & W) • Private Lockers (M & W) •
Golf Lessons • Club Repair •
Memberships

Rental Equipment

	9 holes	18 holes
Carts	$8.00	$16.00

Course Description – A favorite site for state championship tournaments. *Golf Digest* rated this as one of the top five courses in Kentucky in 1989. Renowned treachery is found on 8, a 466-yard dogleg left which has a forked stream running through it in two places.

1992 Champions –
Men's – Joe Pavoni   Senior – Jack Ragsdale
Women's – Martha Humin

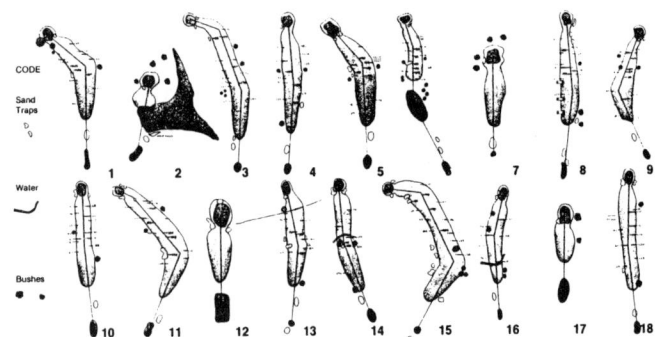

Tees:	Black	White	Gold	Red
PAR:	72	72	72	76
Yardage:	6923	6679	5791	5225
Rating:	74.0	72.9	68.8	70.7
Slope Rating:	133	131	123	123

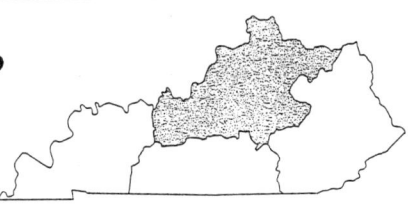

Nevel Meade Golf Club
10509 Highway 329
Prospect, Kentucky
502-228-9522

Location – Right on Covered Bridge Road off Brownsboro Road, past Prospect.

Public	
Year Round – 18 Holes	
Pro – Jere Pelletier, PGA	

Greens Fees
Weekdays $14.50
Evenings $8.50
Weekends $16.50

Facilities/Services Available
  Pro Shop • Driving Range •
  Putting Green • Snack Bar •
  Golf Lessons • Club Repair •
  Group Play • Memberships

Rental Equipment

	9 holes	18 holes
Carts	$10.00	$17.00
Pull Carts	$1.50	$3.00
Golf Clubs	$5.00	$10.00

Course Description – Designed after Scottish Links courses with bent grass tees, fairways and greens. Challenge increased with lots of sand bunkers.

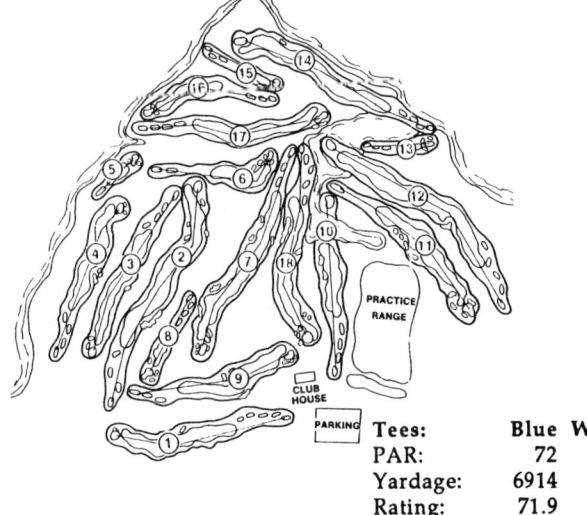

Tees:	Blue	White	Red
PAR:	72	72	72
Yardage:	6914	6516	5474
Rating:	71.9	69.4	68.9
Slope Rating:	119	114	112

Sleepy Hollow Golf Club

4221 South Highway 1694
Prospect, Kentucky
502-241-4475

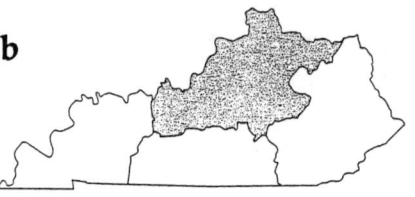

Location – Fifteen miles east of Louisville on Highway 1694S, between Highways 22 and 329 in Oldham County.

Public
March thru November – 9 Holes
Owner – James A. McWilliams

Greens Fees
Weekdays $11.00
Evenings $11.00
Weekends $12.00

Facilities/Services Available
Pro Shop • Driving Range •
Putting Green • Snack Bar

Rental Equipment

	9 holes	18 holes
Carts	$8.00	$16.00
Pull Carts	$1.00	$1.00
Golf Clubs	$1.50	$2.00

Course Description – Gently rolling, wide fairways are of medium length. The course has very few bunkers. A pond is located at the edge of the green on 8, the longest hole, a 577-yard par 5.

Tees:	Blue	Red
PAR:	36	37
Yardage:	3206	2960
Rating:	69.8	72.5

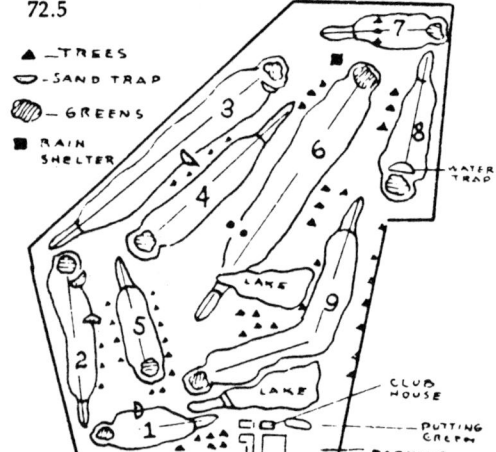

Arlington Golf Center
West Main Street
Richmond, Kentucky
606-622-2207

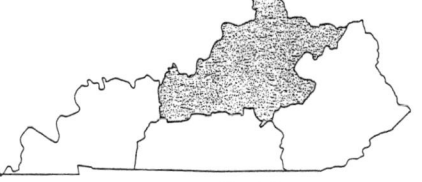

Location – One and one-half miles from exit 90A off I-75.

Private
Year Round – 18 Holes
Pro – Lew Smither, PGA

Greens Fees Guests
Weekdays $15.00
Weekends $20.00

Facilities/Services Available
Pro Shop • Driving Range •
Putting Green • Chipping
Green • Practice Bunker •
Snack Bar • Dining Room •
Meeting Room • Dressing
Rooms (M & W) • Showers (M
& W) • Private Lockers (M &
W) • Golf Lessons • Club
Repair • Memberships

Rental Equipment

	9 holes	18 holes
Carts	$7.00	$14.00
Pull Carts	$2.00	$2.00
Golf Clubs	$7.00	$7.00

Course Description – A hilly plane is engulfed with trees. Five
water holes are a nuisance, especially 4 and 5. Strategically-
placed bunkers also pose threats.

1992 Champions –
Men's – Bill Jennings
Women's – Joni Stephens

Senior – Chuck VandeLune
Junior – Etan Waterbury
Mary Harris

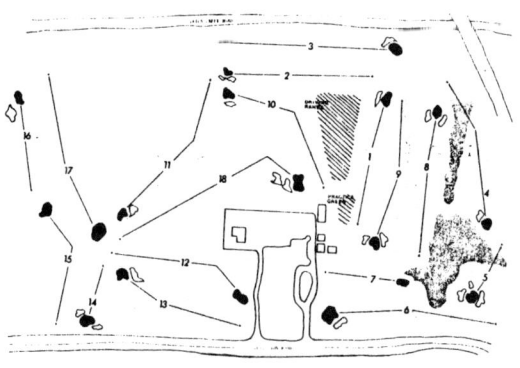

Tees:	Blue	White	Red
PAR:	72	72	72
Yardage:	6486	6156	5422
Rating:	71.5	69.5	71.3
Slope Rating:	119	113	103

Gibson Bay Golf Course

2000 Gibson Bay Drive
Richmond, Kentucky
606-623-0225

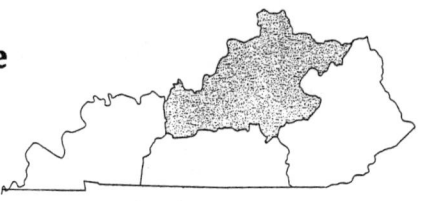

Location – Richmond Exit 87, E.K.U. By-Pass, Right on Gibson Bay Drive 1/2 mile.

Public
18 Holes
Pro – Pat Stephens, PGA

Greens Fees Approximately
Weekdays $10.00
Evenings $6.00
Weekends $14.00

Facilities/Services Available
  Pro Shop • Driving Range •
  Putting Green • Chipping
  Green • Practice Bunker •
  Snack Bar • Golf Lessons •
  Club Repair • Group Play

Rental Equipment

	9 holes	18 holes
Carts	$8.50	$17.00
Pull Carts	$2.00	$4.00
Golf Clubs	$9.00	$9.00

Course Description – A new premier public course. This city owned golf course designed by Michael Hurzdan Design Group of Columbus, Ohio, is around 70 acre lake with 5 tee boxes per hole.

Tees:	Blue	White	Red
PAR:	72	72	72
Yardage:	7113	6508	5069
Rating:	74.1	71.3	69.1
Slope Rating:	128	122	115

Madison Country Club

Red House Road
Richmond, Kentucky
606-623-6468

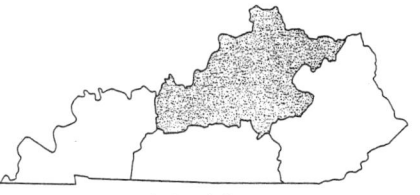

Location – One mile off Main Street on North 2nd Street.

Private
Year Round – 9 Holes
Pro – Danny Hiatt, PGA

Greens Fees Guests
Weekdays $12.00
Weekends $16.00

Facilities/Services Available
Pro Shop • Driving Range •
Putting Green • Chipping
Green • Snack Bar • Dining
Room • Meeting Room •
Meeting Room • Dressing
Rooms (M & W) • Showers (M
& W) • Private Lockers (M & W)
• Golf Lessons • Club Repair
• Memberships

Rental Equipment

	9 holes	18 holes
Carts	$4.00	$8.00

Course Description – A third of the nine holes extend beyond
500 yards. Water must be overshot on five holes. Greens are
small and well-protected by sizable bunkers. Trap on 9 is
located on the right side of a two tiered green, making it one
tough par 3!

1991 Champions –
Men's – Edwin Luxon, Jr.
Women's – Dina Thornberry

Course Record –
9 Holes Edwin Luxon 29
18 Holes Edwin Luxon 62

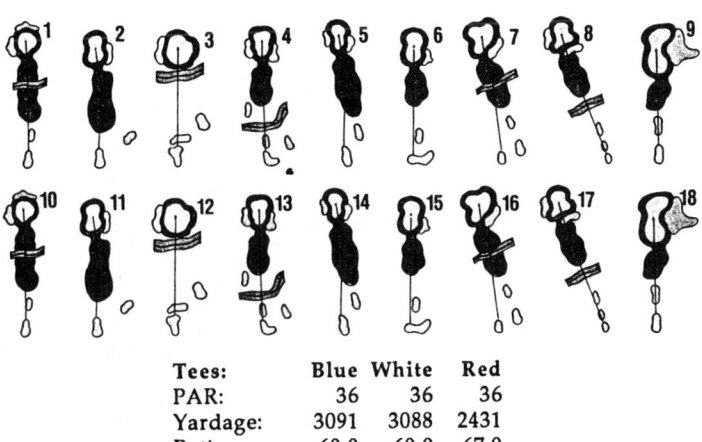

Tees:	Blue	White	Red
PAR:	36	36	36
Yardage:	3091	3088	2431
Rating:	69.9	69.9	67.9
Slope Rating:	114	114	108

Shelbyville Country Club
Smithfield Road
Shelbyville, Kentucky
502-633-0542

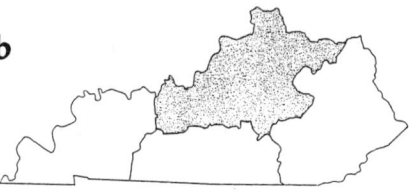

Location – Three-quarter mile north of U.S. 60.

Private
Year Round – 18 Holes
Golf Pro – Dan Iceman

Greens Fees Guests
Weekdays $12.00
Weekends $18.00

Facilities/Services Available
Pro Shop • Driving Range •
Putting Green • Lounge •
Meeting Room • Dressing
Rooms (M & W) • Showers (M
& W) • Private Lockers (M & W)
• Golf Lessons • Club Repair
• Group Play • Memberships

Rental Equipment

	9 holes	**18 holes**
Carts	$8.00	$16.00
Golf Clubs	$5.00	$10.00

Course Description – Built in the mid-1930's, these links offer
the interest of varied layouts. A U-shaped lake wraps
around six holes. The fairway on 18 is essentially water.

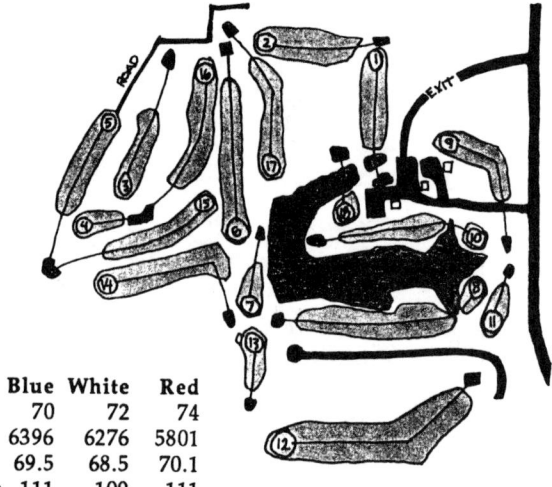

Tees:	Blue	White	Red
PAR:	70	72	74
Yardage:	6396	6276	5801
Rating:	69.5	68.5	70.1
Slope Rating:	111	109	111

Weissinger Hills Golf Course (Formerly Undalata)

224 Mt. Eden Road
Shelbyville, Kentucky
502-633-7332

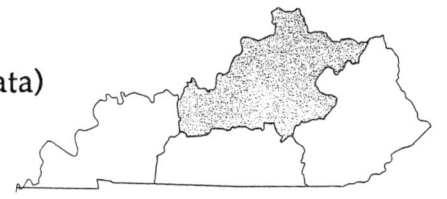

Location – I-64 and Highway 53 (exit 35) Shelbyville.

Public
Year Round – 18 Holes
Pro – Daniel J. Hilker, PGA

Greens Fees
Weekdays	$10.00
Evenings	$7.00
Weekends	$17.00

Facilities/Services Available
Pro Shop • Driving Range •
Putting Green • Chipping
Green • Practice Bunker •
Snack Bar • Lounge • Golf
Lessons • Club Repair •
Group Play • Memberships

Rental Equipment
	18 holes
Carts	$16.00
Pull Carts	$3.00
Golf Clubs	$5.00

Course Description – This course makes the most of the
undulating terrain on which it is built. Each hole offers
challenge and reward for the averager golfer. The clubhouse
is a restored historic mule barn.

Tees:	Gold	Blue	White	Red
PAR:	72	72	72	72
Yardage:	6534	6206	5899	5171
Rating:	70.8	69.3	67.9	69
Slope Rating:	118	115	112	112

Maplehurst Golf Course
700 Bells Mill Road
Shepherdsville, Kentucky
502-957-3370

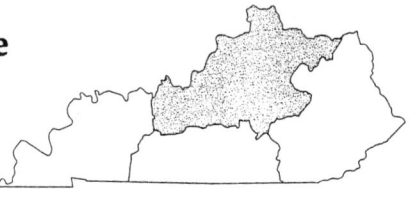

Pubic
18 Holes
Manager – Sammy Tilford

Greens Fees
Weekdays	$7.00
Weekends	$8.00

Facilities/Services Available
Pro Shop • Putting Green •
Snack Bar

Rental Equipment

	9 holes	18 holes
Carts	$8.50	$14.90
Pull Carts	$1.05	$1.05
Golf Clubs	$3.50	$3.50

Course Description – Water is the major threat on this course, interesting nos. 2, 3, 4, 7 and 9. No. 7 is a gigantic 560-yard slight dogleg right with water intimidating tee shots.

Tees:	Blue	White	Red
PAR:	70	70	70
Yardage:	6065	5165	5831
Rating:	67.7		66.3

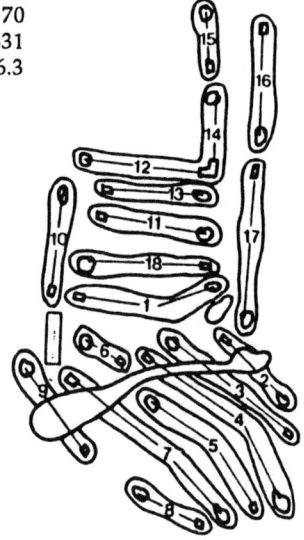

Lincoln Homestead State Park
Route 1
Springfield, Kentucky
606-336-7461

Location – Five miles north of Springfield on State Road 528.

Public **Year Round – 18 Holes** **Pro – Gary Feldman, PGA**	**Greens Fees** Weekdays $15.00 Evenings $7.50 Weekends $15.00 Kentucky State Parks pass program.

Facilities/Services Available
Pro Shop • Driving Range •
Putting Green • Snack Bar •
Meeting Room • Dressing
Rooms (M & W) • Showers (M
& W) • Private Lockers (M & W)
• Golf Lessons • Club Repair
• Group Play • Memberships

Rental Equipment

	9 holes	18 holes
Carts	$8.50	$15.00
Pull Carts	$2.00	$2.00
Golf Clubs	$5.00	$5.00

Course Description – This rolling course is armed with
bunkered, small greens. Fairways are wide and typically
straight. Four holes, however, bend in slight doglegs. Tee
times are suggested from April through October.

1992 Champions –
Men's – Skeeter Leake   Senior – W. F. Simms
Women's – Ina Hamilton   Junior – Matthew Smith

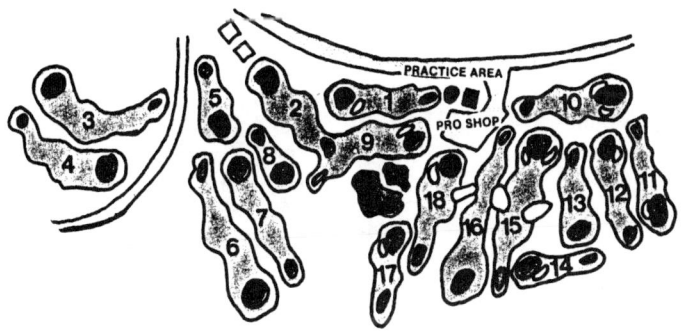

Tees:	Blue	White	Red
PAR:	71	71	75
Yardage:	6359	6350	5677
Rating:	70.7	69.8	70.8
Slope Rating:	119	118	118

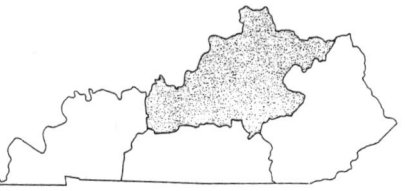

Dix River Country Club
Lancaster Road, Highway 27
Stanford, Kentucky
606-365-2847

Location – Four miles north of Highway 150.

Private	Greens Fees Guests	
Closed January – 18 Holes	Weekdays	$15.00
Golf Pro – Johnnie Tinnat, PGA	Weekends	$20.00

Facilities/Services Available
Pro Shop • Driving Range •
Putting Green • Chipping
Green • Practice Bunker •
Snack Bar • Dining Room •
Dressing Rooms (M & W) •
Showers (M & W) • Private
Lockers (M & W) • Golf
Lessons • Club Repair •
Memberships

Rental Equipment

	9 holes	18 holes
Carts	$3.50	$7.00
Pull Carts	$1.00	$1.00
Golf Clubs	$5.00	$5.00

Course Description – Although the course reads short on the card, scores may be long. The fairways are very hilly, so level lies are not a part of the game here. Undulating greens are better than average.

1992 Champions –
Men's – Charles Hester   Junior – David Horesman, Jr.
Women's – Jessica Cornelius

Tees:	Blue	White	Red
PAR:	72	72	72
Yardage:	6317	5781	4642
Rating:	68.7	67.5	66.3
Slope Rating:	116	113	108

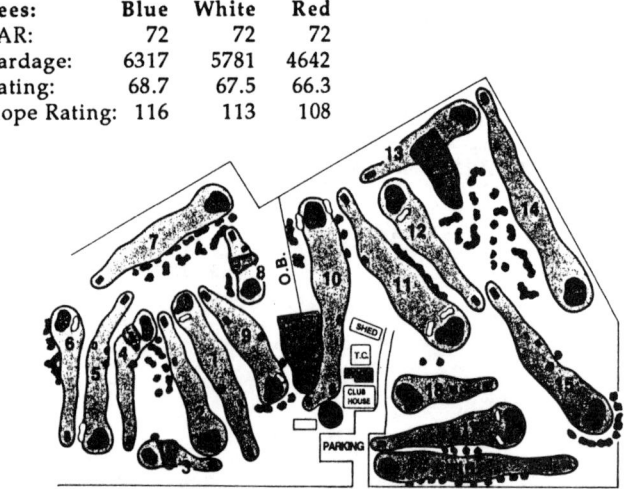

Tanglewood Golf Course
Highway 44E
Taylorsville, Kentucky
502-477-2468

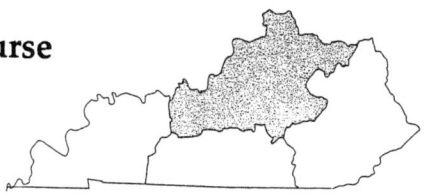

Location – Two miles east of Taylorsville on Highway 44.

Semi-Private

Year Round – 18 Holes

Pro – George S. Sullivan, PGA

Greens Fees
Weekdays $8.00
Weekends $13.00

Facilities/Services Available
Pro Shop • Putting Green •
Chipping Green • Snack Bar •
Golf Lessons • Club Repair •
Group Play • Memberships

Rental Equipment

	9 holes	18 holes
Carts	$10.00	$17.00
Pull Carts	$3.00	$3.00

Course Description – Rolling hills add to the challenge, while tight, tree-lined fairways, four water hazards and elevated greens place a premium on accuracy throughout.

1992 Champions –
Men's – Sam Whitakes

Tees:	Blue	White	Red
PAR:	72	72	72
Yardage:	6414	6053	5723
Rating:	70.2	68.6	68.8
Slope Rating:	121	118	115

Triple Crown Country Club

1 Triple Crown Blvd.
Union, Kentucky
606-384-1220

Location – 20 miles south of Cincinnati, Ohio. On I-75 South take the Richwood, Kentucky exit. Turn right, course is one-half mile on right.

Private	
18 Holes	
Director of Golf – Wayne A. Oien	

Greens Fees	Guests
Weekdays	$25.00
Evenings	$25.00
Weekends	$30.00

Facilities/Services Available
Pro Shop • Driving Range •
Putting Green • Chipping Green
• Practice Bunker • Snack Bar •
Dining Room • Lounge • Meeting
Room • Dressing Rooms (M & W)
• Showers (M & W) • Private
Lockers (M & W) • Golf Lessons •
Club Repair • Memberships

Rental Equipment

	9 holes	18 holes
Carts	$10.00	$20.00

Course Description – Rated as the thirteenth best new course in America in 1992. Rolling hills, holes carved through the woods, many shots over water, and demanding length all describe this course.

1992 Champions –
Men's – Bob Schaar
Women's – Mary Beth Kenning

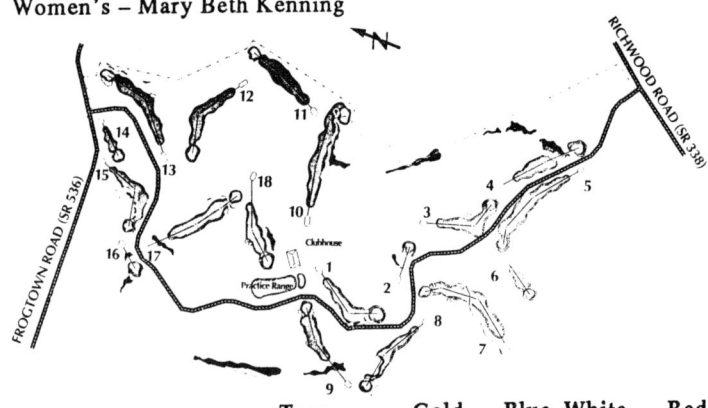

Tees:	Gold	Blue	White	Red
PAR:	72	72	72	72
Yardage:	7108	6674	6155	5269
Rating:	74.5	72.5	70.1	
Slope Rating:	139	131	124	

Sun Valley Golf Course

6505 Bethany Lane
Valley Station, Kentucky
502-937-9228

Location – One mile from Dixie Highway, west end of Gene Snyder Freeway.

Public
Year Round – 9 Holes
Pro – Barry Basham, PGA

Greens Fees

Weekdays	$7.00
Evenings	$5.00
Weekends	$8.00

Facilities/Services Available
Pro Shop • Driving Range •
Putting Green • Chipping
Green • Practice Bunker •
Snack Bar • Showers (M) •
Private Lockers (M) • Golf
Lessons • Club Repair •
Group Play

Rental Equipment

	9 holes	18 holes
Carts	$9.00	$16.00
Pull Carts	$2.00	$1.00
Golf Clubs	$3.00	$3.00

Course Description – The setting here is relatively flat and easy to walk. Nos. 1 and 2 are the only doglegs on the course. Most greens have a moderate amount of sand.

1992 Champions –
Men's – Bob Parrish

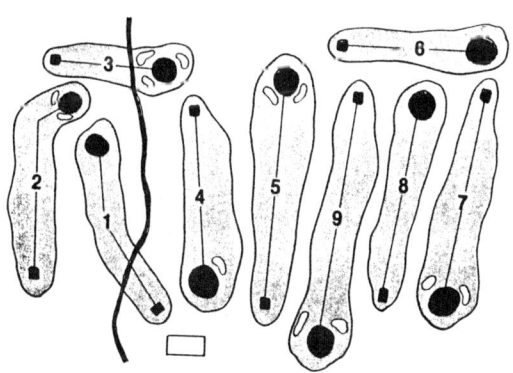

Tees:	Blue	White	Red
PAR:	35	35	38
Yardage:	3137	3045	2600
Rating:	68.6		78.4
Slope Rating:	100		103

Cabin Brook Golf Club

2260 Lexington Road
Versailles, Kentucky
606-873-8404

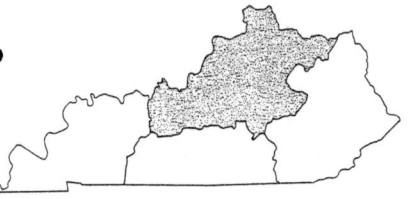

Location – Seven miles from New Circle Road in Lexington on U. S. 60.

Public

Year Round – 18 Holes

Pro – Kenneth Hall, PGA

    Mike Ernest, PGA

Greens Fees
Weekdays $10.00
Weekends $12.00
Pass programs available.

Facilities/Services Available
Pro Shop • Driving Range •
Putting Green • Chipping
Green • Practice Bunker •
Snack Bar • Golf Lessons •
Club Repair • Group Play •
Memberships

Rental Equipment

	9 holes	18 holes
Carts	$8.00	$16.00
Pull Carts	$.50	$1.00
Golf Clubs	$3.50	$5.00

Course Description – Thirteen holes exceed 400 yards on this long course. Two lakes are threaded by streams, and water has a monstrous presence on five holes. Traps await misplaced balls throughout.

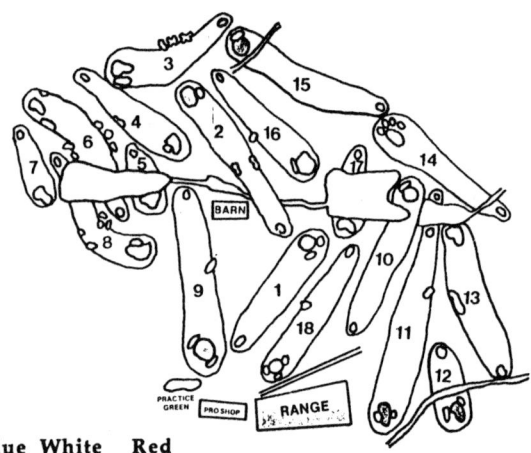

Tees:	Blue	White	Red
PAR:	72	72	72
Yardage:	7027	6332	5183
Rating:	72.4	69.1	68.3
Slope Rating:	117	110	108

Woodford Hills Country Club

Route 3
Versailles, Kentucky
606-873-8122

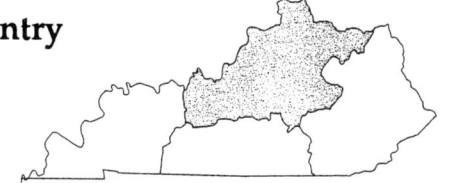

Location – Two miles south of Versailles.

Semi-Private
Year Round – 18 Holes
General Manager – Wilbur Moffett

Greens Fees Guests
Weekdays $16.00
Weekends $18.00

Facilities/Services Available
  Pro Shop • Driving Range •
  Putting Green • Snack Bar •
  Dining Room • Meeting Room
  • Dressing Rooms (M & W) •
  Showers (M & W) • Private
  Lockers (M & W) • Golf
  Lessons • Group Play •
  Memberships

Rental Equipment
	9 holes	18 holes
Carts	$7.00	$14.00

Course Description – This course has the elements on most
Buck Blankenship designs. Gently rolling hills are the
natural setting. Five water hazards and sand traps throughout create perils.

1992 Champions –
Men's – Nate Hollon   Senior – Granville Egbert
Women's – Tracye Furlong

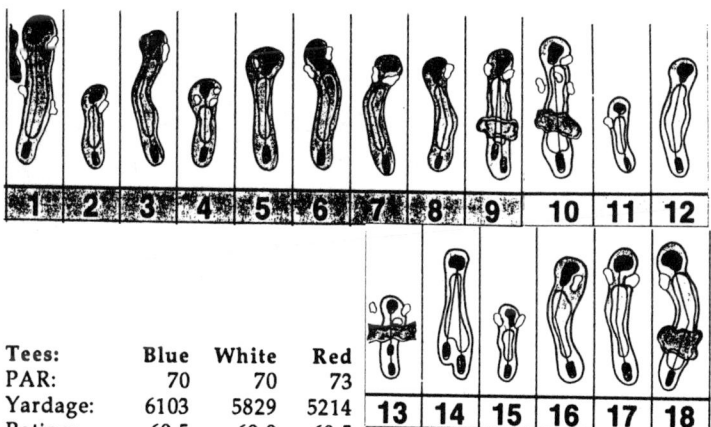

Tees:	Blue	White	Red
PAR:	70	70	73
Yardage:	6103	5829	5214
Rating:	69.5	69.9	69.5
Slope Rating:	118	118	118

Lincoln Trail Country Club

900 Greenhill Road
Vine Grove, Kentucky
502-877-2181

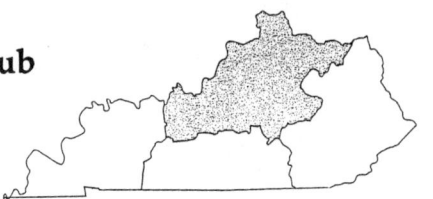

Location – Follow 313 out of Radcliff to the end; turn left on 144.

Semi-Private

Year Round – 18 Holes

Pro – Bob Fraley, PGA

Greens Fees
Weekdays $12.00
Weekends $17.00

Facilities/Services Available
Pro Shop • Driving Range •
Putting Green • Chipping
Green • Snack Bar • Dressing
Rooms (M & W) • Golf Lessons
• Club Repair • Group Play •
Memberships

Rental Equipment

	9 holes	18 holes
Carts	$10.00	$18.00

Course Description – This beautifully-landscaped, park-like course atmosphere is not as innocent as it looks. Water disjoints five holes, and forestry rewards accuracy only.

1	2	3	4	5	6	7	8	9

10	11	12	13	14	15	16	17	18

Tees:	Blue	White	Red
PAR:	72	72	72
Yardage:	6618	6271	5302
Rating:	70.6	69.8	69.9
Slope Rating:	122	120	117

Sugar Bay Golf Course
Dry Creek Road
Warsaw, Kentucky
800-428-0278

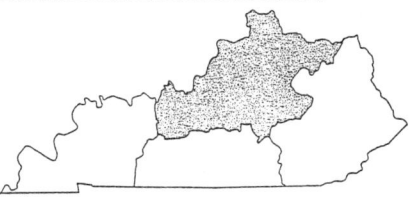

Location – North on I-71 to Exit 57, go left on Sparta Pike (35) 5.8 miles. Go right on Dry Creek Road, one mile on left.

Semi-Private
18 Holes
Director of Golf – T. Bruce Oldendick

Greens Fees
Weekdays $10.00
Evenings $10.00
Weekends $10.00
$11.00 with cart for Seniors
Monday thru Wednesday.

Facilities/Services Available
   Pro Shop • Putting Green •
   Chipping Green • Snack Bar •
   Dining Room • Golf Lessons •
   Club Repair • Group Play •
   Memberships

Rental Equipment

	9 holes	18 holes
Carts	$5.00	$7.00
Pull Carts	$2.00	$2.00
Golf Clubs	$4.00	$4.00

Course Description – Course is very challenging for all handicaps. Fairly flat, but tight with many lakes and trees. Ohio River setting.

1992 Champions –
Men's – George Higdon   Senior – Tom Oldendick
Women's – Lori Oldendick   Junior – Layne Miles

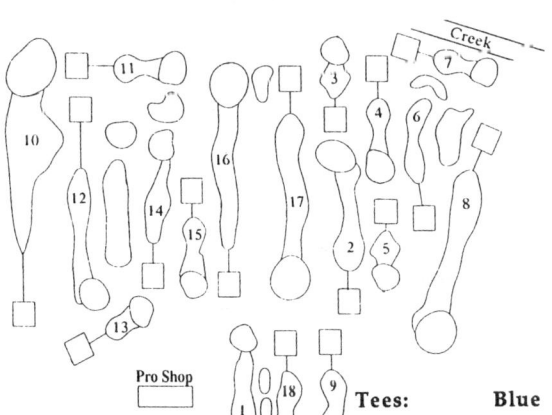

Tees:	Blue	White	Red
PAR:	70	70	70
Yardage:	6144	5804	5282
Rating:	67.0	66.4	67.4
Slope Rating:	106	105	106

Fairway Golf Course
Highway 227
Wheatley, Kentucky
502-463-2338

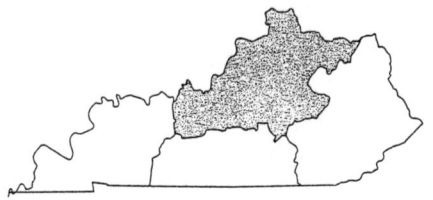

Location – Twelve miles south of I-71, Carrollton exit.

Public
Year Round – 18 Holes
Golf Pro – Gilbert England

Greens Fees
Weekdays $7.00
Weekends $9.00

Facilities/Services Available
Pro Shop • Driving Range •
Putting Green • Snack Bar •
Meeting Room • Golf Lessons
• Club Repair • Group Play

Rental Equipment

	9 holes	18 holes
Carts	$7.00	$14.00
Pull Carts	$.50	$1.00

Course Description – Parallel fairways are straight for the most part. Water comes into play on five holes, including a major chunk of 18.

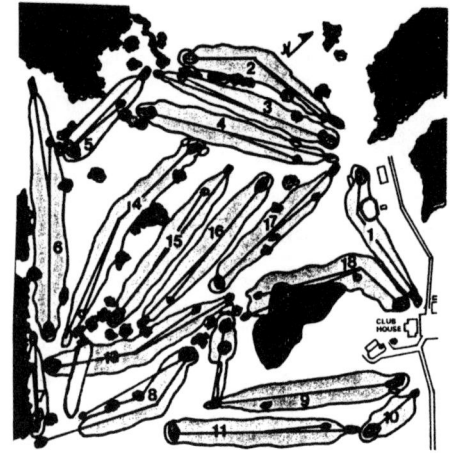

Tees:	Blue	Red
PAR:	70	70
Yardage:	5800	5420
Rating:	66.0	68.9
Slope Rating:	100	101

Southwinds Golf Course

2480 New Boonesboro Road
Winchester, Kentucky
606-744-0375

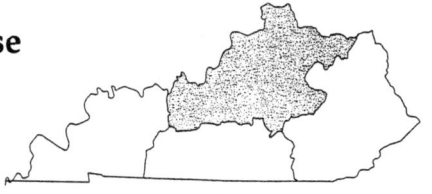

Location – From Winchester right on Boonesboro Road for
one-half mile.

Semi-Private
18 Holes
Manager – Billy Todd

Greens Fees
Weekdays $15.00
Weekends $20.50
Cart included.

Facilities/Services Available
Pro Shop • Driving Range •
Putting Green • Chipping
Green • Snack Bar • Lounge •
Memberships

Course Description – Tough Par 3s are complicated by three
lakes on this new course. Some 250 recently planted seedlings
promise to mature into hazardous scenic beauty.

Tees:	Blue	White	Red
PAR:	71	71	71
Yardage:	6265	6060	4700
Slope Rating:	113	109	116

Winchester Country Club

410 Boone Avenue
Winchester, Kentucky
606-744-4884

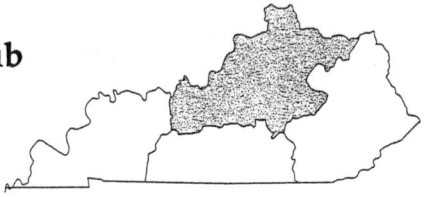

Location – On U.S. 27 near George Rogers Clark High School.

Private	**Greens Fees** Guests
Year Round – 18 Holes	Weekdays $15.00
Pro – Robert Baldwin, PGA	Weekends $25.00

Facilities/Services Available
Pro Shop • Putting Green •
Chipping Green • Practice
Bunker • Snack Bar • Dining
Room • Lounge • Dressing
Rooms (M & W) • Showers (M
& W) • Private Lockers (M &
W) • Golf Lessons • Club
Repair • Memberships

Rental Equipment

	9 holes	18 holes
Carts	$5.00	$8.00
Pull Carts	$.50	

Course Description – Rolling hills feature tight, tree-lined
fairways. Premium is on accuracy, especially around
unforgiving greens. Three water hazards also add to interest
and challenge.

1992 Champions –
Men's – Bob McCann
Women's – Talitha Freeman

Tees:	Blue	White	Red
PAR:	71	71	71
Yardage:	6180	6100	5200
Rating:	68.4	68.4	69.4
Slope Rating:	121	119	117

NORTH CENTRAL APPENDIX

Additional Regulation Courses

Location	Name	Holes	Type	Telephone
Carlisle	15th Hole of Carnico	9	PUB	606-289-7238
Covington	Ryland Lakes C.C.	9	PRI	606-356-9444
Frankfort	Links at Drucker's Lake	18	SPR	502-695-0818
LaGrange	LaGrange Woods	9	SPR	502-222-7927
Lebanon	Lebanon C. C.	9	PRI	502-692-3541
Louisville	Indian Springs G. C.	18	*	502-893-3516
Louisville	Lake Forest C. C.	18	PRI	502-245-6184
Middletown	Midland Trail G. C.	18	PRI	502-245-0223
Paris	Stoner Creek C. C.	9	PRI	606-987-0025
Richmond	Bluegrass Army Depot G.C.	9	SPR	606-623-5852

*Under Construction

Other Golf Facilities

Par Threes (P3)   Executive Course (EC)
Practice Range (PR)

Location	Name	Holes	Type	Telephone
Elizabethtown	American Legion Par 3	9	P3	502-765-4030
Florence	World of Sports	18	EC	502-371-1399
Lexington	Par Three Mason Headly Rd.	9	P3	606-252-8253
Lexington	Meadowbrook Golf	9	P3	606-272-3115
Louisville	Bellarmine Golf Course	9	EC	502-452-8378
Louisville	Bobicks Golf	9	EC	502-964-1867
Louisville	Golf World	9	P3	502-241-6741
Louisville	Golf Experience	–	PR	502-426-0774
Louisville	Practice Tee	–	PR	502-895-4144
Louisville	Southern Sports	–	PR	502-964-4653
Louisville	Shively Par Three	9	P3	502-447-9111
Louisville	Toms	–	PR	502-897-3743
Rough River	Falls State Resort	9	P3	502-257-2311
Shelbyville	Clear Creek	18	EC	502-633-0375
Shepherdsville	Buffalo Run	–	PR	502-543-7483
Valley Station	Golf Etc.	–	PR	502-937-9003
Winchester	Sportland	18	EC	606-744-9959

Eastern Region

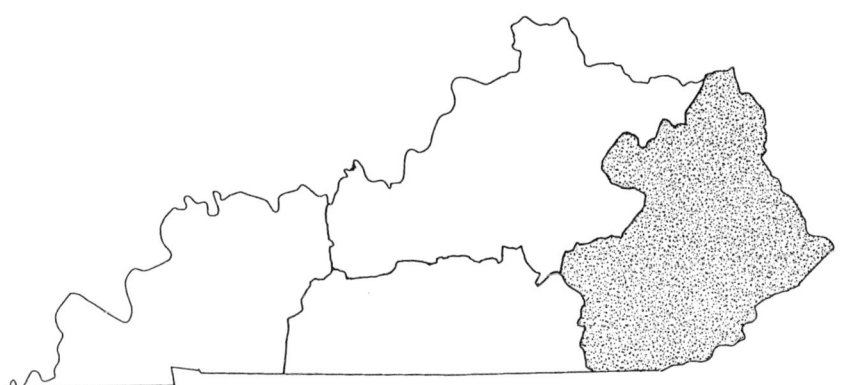

River Bend Golf Club
Route 4
Argillite, Kentucky
606-473-6773

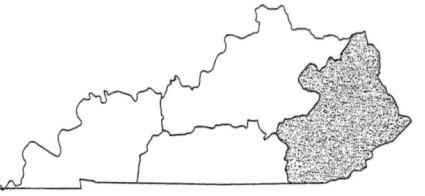

Location – One mile north of Greenbo State Park.

Public	
18 Holes	
Manager – Michael Lucas	

Greens Fees Guests
Weekdays $12.00
Evenings $12.00
Weekends $12.00
Senior Day – Monday &
Thursday

Facilities/Services Available
  Pro Shop •Driving Range •
  Putting Green • Snack Bar •
  Golf Lessons • Memberships

Rental Equipment
                    18 holes
Carts $7.50

Course Description – Located on the Little Sandy River, this offers something for every skill level. It's a flat, challenging course with lots of water, five tee levels, bent grass tees and irrigated greens.

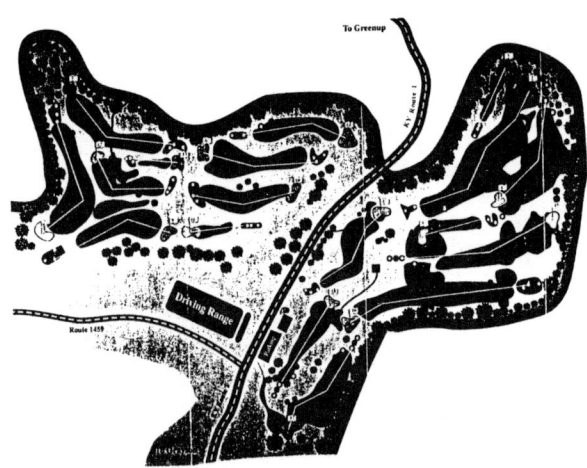

Tees:	Blue	White	Red
PAR:	72	72	72
Yardage:	6042	5552	4338

Bellefonte Country Club

208 Country Club Drive
Ashland, Kentucky
606-329-1966

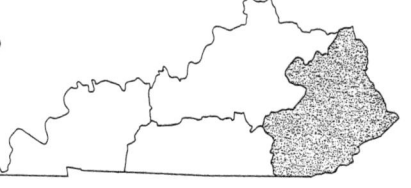

Location – Three miles west of town on Highway 23, turn on Route 5.

Private
Year Round – 18 Holes
Pro – Jack Freeman, PGA

Greens Fees Guests
Weekdays $25.00
Weekends $25.00

Facilities/Services Available
Pro Shop •Driving Range •
Putting Green • Chipping Green
• Practice Bunker • Snack Bar
•Dining Room • Lounge •
Meeting Room • Dressing Rooms
(M & W) • Showers (M & W) •
Private Lockers (M & W) • Golf
Lessons • Club Repair

Rental Equipment

	9 holes	18 holes
Carts	$6.50	$13.00

Course Description – Varied layout sharpens both long and short game. Tree-lined, undulating landscape creates a tight outlook for most holes. Only one hole has water.

1992 Champions
Men's – Bill Stinnett
Women's – Ginny Hagans

Senior – Dave Elam
Junior – Houston Fraley
Meg Ehrie

Tees:	Blue	White	Red
PAR:	70	70	71
Yardage:	6060	5896	5049
Rating:	68.4	67.2	68.2
Slope Rating:	108	107	107

Sandy Creek Golf Course
Ashland, Kentucky
606-928-6321

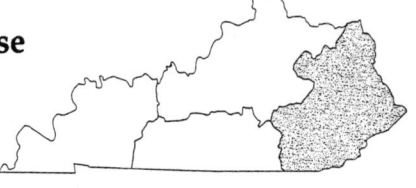

Location – Five miles West of I-64, Cannonsberg exit.

Public
18 Holes
Pro – Richard Mahar, PGA

Greens Fees
Weekdays $11.00
Weekends $13.00

Facilities/Services Available
Pro Shop •Putting Green •
Chipping Green • Practice
Bunker • Snack Bar • Golf
Lessons • Club Repair •
Group Play • Memberships

Rental Equipment

	9 holes	18 holes
Carts	$4.00	$8.00
Pull Carts	$1.50	

Course Description – Flat, short, good walking course. Creek meanders throughout this entire heavily wooded course.

1992 Champions –
Men's – Mike Wood

Tees:	Blue
PAR:	70
Yardage:	5744

Indian Springs Country Club
Kentucky Highway 6
Barbourville, Kentucky
606-546-5607

Location – Four miles west of Barbourville, on Kentucky Highway 6.

Semi-Private	
Year Round – 9 Holes	

Greens Fees
Weekdays $7.00
Weekends $10.00

Facilities/Services Available
Putting Green • Snack Bar •
Meeting Room • Club Repair •
Memberships

Rental Equipment

	9 holes	18 holes
Carts	$10.00	$12.00

Course Description – A maze of long holes (four over 400 yards) demands a consistent swing. No. 2 is a mammoth 598-yard slight dogleg left. The tee on 3 overlooks water, which also appears on 15 and 16.

1992 Champions
Men's – Ron Phipps

Tees:	Blue	White	Red
PAR:	36	36	36
Yardage:	3188	3064	2810
Rating:	71.5	70.7	73.2

Bear Creek Country Club

Rt. 180
Catlettsburg, Kentucky
606-928-5335

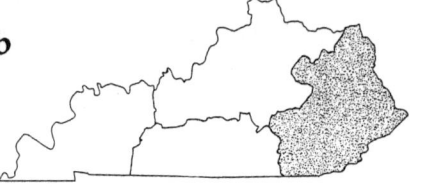

Location – Take exit 185 on I-64; go south on Route 180.

Public	
18 Holes	
Manager – Tom Mouilso	

Greens Fees Guests
Weekdays $16.00
Weekends $19.00

Facilities/Services Available
Pro Shop • Putting Green •
Snack Bar •Group Play •
Memberships

Rental Equipment
                        9 holes 18 holes
Carts   Included in Green Fee

Course Description – This long and challenging course is toughened with interfering bunkers and trees.

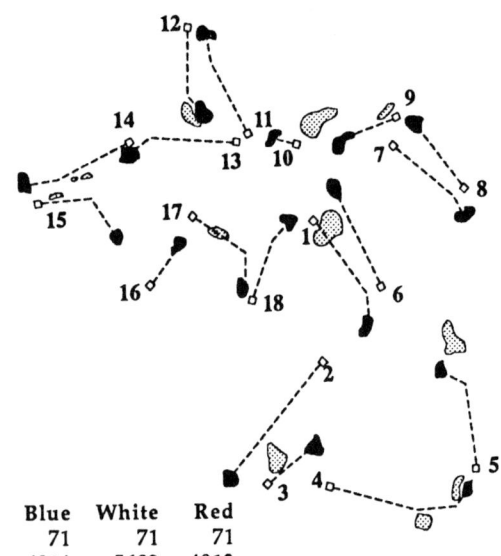

Tees:	Blue	White	Red
PAR:	71	71	71
Yardage:	6014	5602	4913
Slope Rating:	118		

Rolling Meadows Country Club

Catlettsburg, Kentucky
606-739-4140

Location – Cannonburg exit off I-64, go north on St. R. 60; right on Shopes Creek.

Public
9 Holes
Owner – Robert Craycraft

Greens Fees Guests
Weekdays $7.00
Weekends $8.00

Facilities/Services Available
Pro Shop • Putting Green •
Snack Bar • Dining Room •
Group Play • Memberships

Rental Equipment

	9 holes	18 holes
Carts	$6.36	$11.00

Course Description – This very hilly course has an intimidating lake on its signature no. 7 hole.

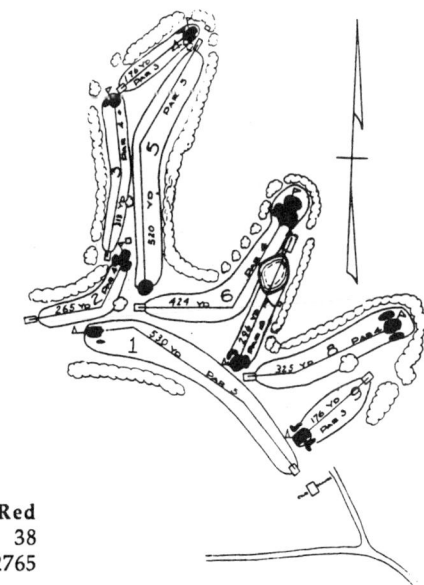

Tees:	Blue	Red
PAR:	36	38
Yardage:	3045	2765

Cole Park Golf Club

1601 Lee Road
Fort Campbell, Kentucky
502-798-4906

Location – Five miles south of I-24 on 41A, 9 miles north-west of Clarksville, Tennessee.

Military
Year Round – 18 Holes
Pro – Mike DiPasquale, PGA

Greens Fees

	Guests/Public
Weekdays	$14.00
Evenings	$8.00
Weekends	$14.00

Facilities/Services Available
Pro Shop • Driving Range • Putting Green • Chipping Green • Practice Bunker • Snack Bar • Dining Room • Meeting Room • Dressing Rooms (M & W) • Showers (M & W) • Private Lockers (M) • Golf Lessons • Club Repair • Group Play • Memberships

Rental Equipment

	9 holes	18 holes
Carts	$7.00	$14.00
Pull Carts	$3.00	$3.00
Golf Clubs	$5.00	$5.00

Course Description – The well-conditioned, picturesque course puts up a fight all the way. Bent grass greens are large and armed with bunkers. Sand is a hassle throughout, but there are only two water hazards.

1992 Champions
Men's – Sam Cross

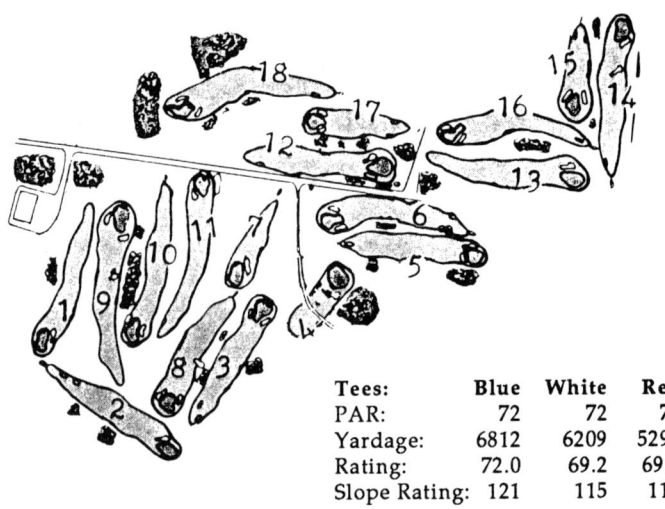

Tees:	Blue	White	Red
PAR:	72	72	72
Yardage:	6812	6209	5296
Rating:	72.0	69.2	69.6
Slope Rating:	121	115	116

Crooked Creek Golf Club

781 Crooked Creek Drive
London, Kentucky
606-877-1993

Location – I-75 to Exit 38, east on Highway 192, at sixth
light, turn right and follow signs.

Semi-Private

18 Holes

Pro – Bill R. Moore, PGA

Greens Fees Guests/Public
Weekdays $27.50
Evenings $27.50
Weekends $27.50
Forecard, pre-payment 4
rounds cart & GF $100.00

Facilities/Services Available
Pro Shop •Driving Range •
Putting Green • Chipping
Green • Practice Bunker •
Snack Bar • Golf Lessons •
Club Repair • Group Play •
Memberships

Rental Equipment
              9 holes 18 holes
Carts $5.00 $10.00

Course Description – 18 hole championship course has a great
variety of valley, linkish, mountain, and low country wooded
holes, along with contoured, mounded fairways and greens.
Rounds also feature five sets of tees, beautiful, scenic green
settings and course vistas.

Tees:	Blue	White	Red
PAR:	72	72	72
Yardage:	7007	6400	5700

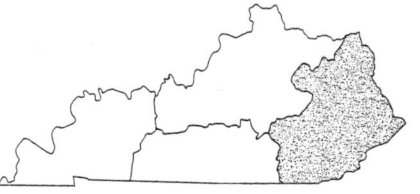

London Country Club
835 West Laurel Road
London, Kentucky
606-864-2282

Location – About a mile west on I-75 on Highway 192.

Private
Year Round – 18 Holes
Pro – Scott Mishler, PGA

Greens Fees Guests
Weekdays $20.00
Weekends $20.00

Facilities/Services Available
Pro Shop • Driving Range •
Putting Green • Chipping
Green • Snack Bar • Lounge •
Meeting Room • Golf Lessons
• Club Repair • Memberships

Rental Equipment

	9 holes	18 holes
Carts	$5.00	$10.00
Golf Clubs	$4.00	$8.00

Course Description – Carved out of hills, this course is largely wooded and includes four water hazards. No. 4 is over water for the most part. Fairways and greens are generous.

Tees:	Blue	White	Red
PAR:	71	71	71
Yardage:	6424	5716	5037
Rating:	69.9	66.6	67.8
Slope Rating:	112	106	107

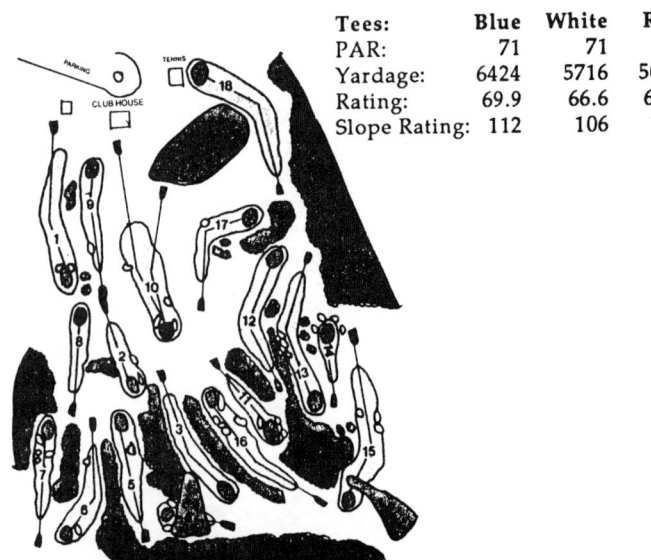

Sweet Hollow Resort
U. S. 25 W
London, Kentucky
606-523-1241

Location – I-75 at Corbin, exit 29, four miles NE on Highway 25.

Public
9 Holes
Pro – Luther Minor Jr., PGA

Greens Fees Guests
Weekdays $10.00
Weekends $12.00

Facilities/Services Available
Pro Shop • Driving Range •
Putting Green • Chipping
Green • Snack Bar • Dining
Room • Dressing Rooms (M &
W) • Showers (M & W) •
Private Lockers (M & W) • Golf
Lessons • Club Repair • Group
Play • Memberships

Rental Equipment

	9 holes	18 holes
Carts	$4.25	$8.50

Course Description – This challenging, wooded playing field has water everywhere – 16 lakes in all!

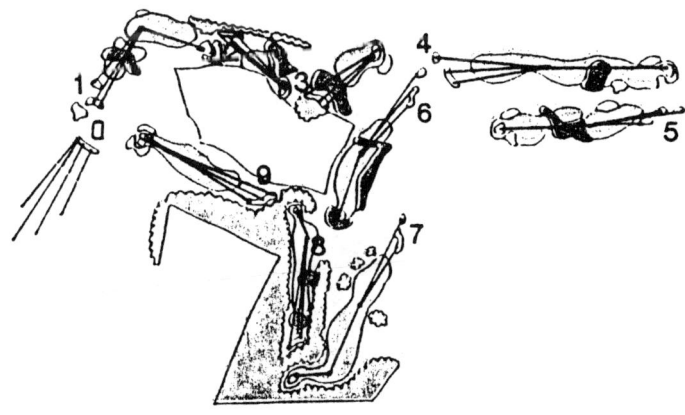

Tees:	Blue	White	Red
PAR:	36	36	36
Yardage:	3240	3022	2649

The Lakes Golf Club
Route 7
Maloneton, Kentucky
606-932-4266

Location – Five miles south of South Shore.

Public	
March thru December – 9 Holes	
Owner – Stan Timberlake	

Greens Fees

Weekdays	$5.00
Evenings	$5.00
Weekends	$6.00

Pass programs available.

Facilities/Services Available
Pro Shop • Putting Green •
Chipping Green • Snack Bar •
Dining Room • Dressing
Rooms (M & W) • Private
Lockers (M & W) • Club
Repair • Group Play • Memberships

Rental Equipment

	9 holes	18 holes
Carts	$8.00	$16.00
Pull Carts	$1.00	$2.00
Golf Clubs	$3.00	$5.00

Course Description – Rolling fairways are tree-laden. Tee boxes are arranged and fairways are designed in a way that creates a separate back nine. Water is a serious factor on six holes.

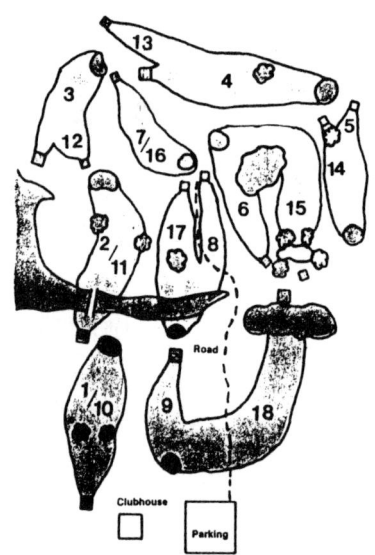

Tees:	Blue
PAR:	35
Yardage:	3100

Big Hickory Golf Course
Manchester, Kentucky
606-598-8053

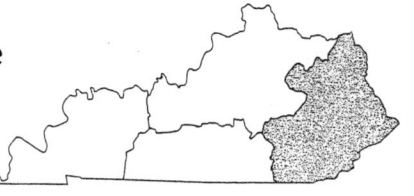

Location – Located 2 miles northeast of Manchester.

Public
Year Round – 9 Holes
Owner – Zenith Campbell

Greens Fees

	9 Holes	18 Holes
Weekdays	$5.00	$8.00
Weekends	$6.00	$10.00

Facilities/Services Available
Pro Shop • Driving Range •
Putting Green • Chipping
Green • Snack Bar • Golf
Lessons • Club Repair • Group
Play

Course Description – This new course has its rigors: narrow fairways and lots of menacingly placed trees.

Tees:	Blue	White	Red
PAR:	36	36	36
Yardage:	5924	5624	5090

Mt. Sterling Golf & Country Club
Highway 460 East
Mt. Sterling, Kentucky
606-498-3142

Location – Mt. Sterling Exit 110, off I-64. Take 686 By-Pass to 460 and turn right.

Private
9 Holes
Pro – Kirk Schooley, PGA

Greens Fees Guests
Weekdays $9.00
Weekends $12.00

Rental Equipment

	9 holes	18 holes
Carts	$7.00	$14.00

Course Description – The course plays to 6,800 yards, and the greens are extremely undulating.

1992 Champions
Men's – Dr. Mike Prunty
Women's – Gayle McCormick

Tees:	Blue	Red
PAR:	72	72
Yardage:	6800	6000
Rating:	68.4	68.2
Slope Rating:	122	119

Carter Caves State Resort Park

Route 5
Olive Hill, Kentucky
606-286-4411

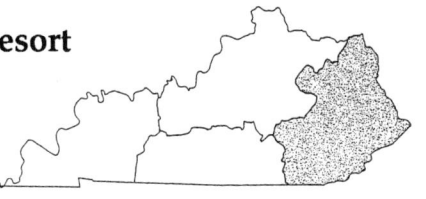

Location – Three miles north of I-64 exit 161.

Public
Year Round – 9 Holes

Greens Fees
Weekdays $10.00
Weekends $10.00
Kentucky State Parks pass program. American Lung Association Cards accepted.

Facilities/Services Available
Pro Shop • Putting Green •
Snack Bar • Group Play

Rental Equipment

	9 holes	18 holes
Carts	$8.50	$15.00
Pull Carts	$1.00	$1.00
Golf Clubs	$5.00	$5.00

Course Description – Set on a hilly terrain, fairways are tight with dense, mature trees. The course has no water.

Tees:	Blue	White	Red
PAR:	35	35	35
Yardage:	2900	2869	2769
Rating:	66.7	66.7	66.7

Mountain Pub-Links

8709 Lower Johns Creek Road
Pikeville, Kentucky
606-437-0339

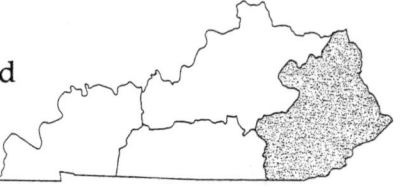

Location – Ten miles southeast of Pikeville on Highway 194.

Public	
Year Round – 9 Holes	
President – Jack Sykes	

Greens Fees
Weekdays $10.00
Evenings $7.00
Weekends $15.00

Facilities/Services Available
 Pro Shop • Putting Green •
 Chipping Green • Snack Bar •
 Golf Lessons • Club Repair •
 Group Play • Memberships

Rental Equipment

	9 holes	18 holes
Carts	$4.00	$8.00
Pull Carts		$1.50
Golf Clubs		$2.00

Course Description – Plush 9-hole course in a solitary environment is surrounded by beautiful mountains. Course is tough enough for a challenging game and yet short enough to enjoy a nice outing.

1992 Champions
Men's – Willie Edelen
Women's – Leslie Combs

Tees:	Blue	Red
PAR:	36	36
Yardage:	2813	2256

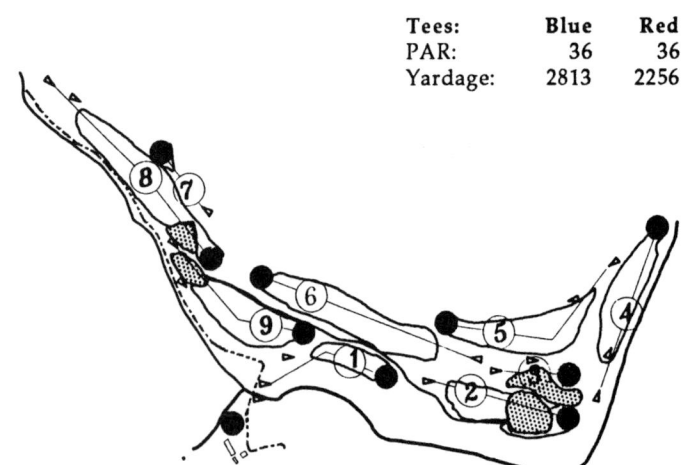

Jenny Wiley State Resort Park
Kentucky Highway 3
Prestonsburg, Kentucky
606-886-2711

Location – Two miles north of Prestonsburg on Highway 3.

Public
Year Round – 9 Holes
Pro Shop Manager – Kristi Faye

Greens Fees
Weekdays $10.00
Evenings $10.00
Weekends $10.00
Kentucky State Parks pass
program. American Lung
Association Cards accepted.

Facilities/Services Available
   Pro Shop • Putting Green •
   Chipping Green • Snack Bar •
   Dining Room • Dressing
   Rooms (M & W) • Golf Lessons
   • Club Repair • Group Play

Rental Equipment

	9 holes	18 holes
Carts	$9.00	$17.00
Pull Carts	$2.00	$2.00
Golf Clubs	$6.00	$6.00

Course Description – This course is laid out on rolling hills.
Narrow fairways are lined with mature trees of all varieties.

1992 Champions
Men's – Gary Brown

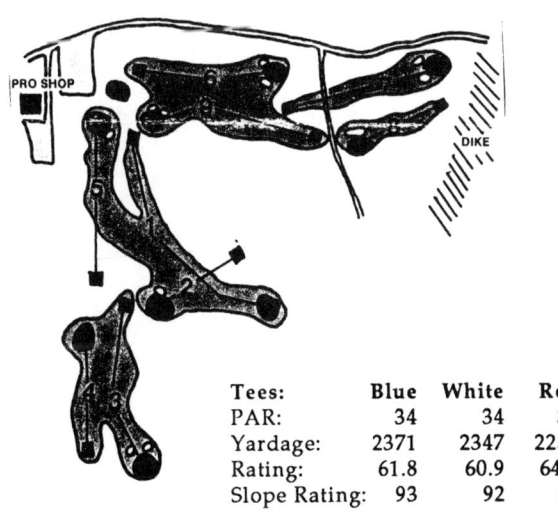

Tees:	Blue	White	Red
PAR:	34	34	34
Yardage:	2371	2347	2235
Rating:	61.8	60.9	64.1
Slope Rating:	93	92	98

Pleasant Valley Country Club

Liberty Road
West Liberty, Kentucky
606-743-9172

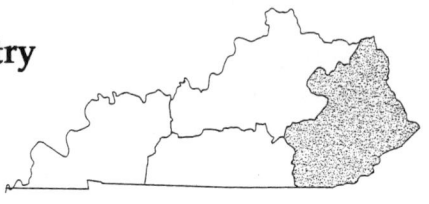

Location – Two miles south of U.S. 460 on Kentucky 2498.

Private
Year Round – 9 Holes
Club Pro/Manager – John Stacy

Greens Fees
Weekdays $10.00
Weekends $15.00

Facilities/Services Available
Pro Shop • Putting Green •
Chipping Green • Snack Bar •
Meeting Room • Dressing
Rooms (M & W) •Showers (M &
W) •Private Lockers (M & W) •
Club Repair • Memberships

Rental Equipment

	9 holes	18 holes
Carts	$4.00	$8.00

Course Description – From tee to green, only one hole exceeds 400 yards. Outlook is hilly and tight, with trees doing more than adding to the scene.

1992 Champions
Men's – John Stacy

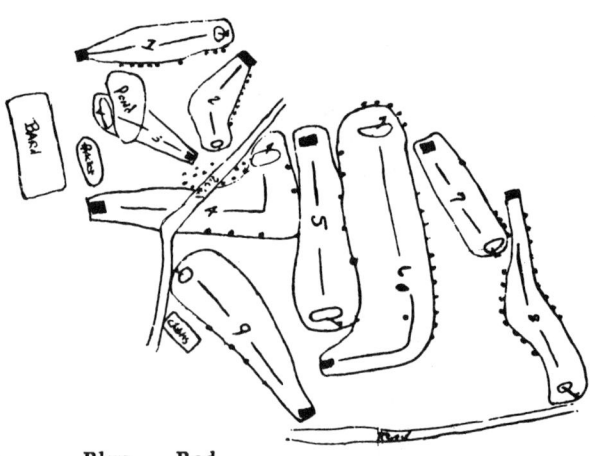

Tees:	Blue	Red
PAR:	35	35
Yardage:	2865	2117

EASTERN APPENDIX

Additional Regulation Courses

Location	Name	Holes	Type	Telephone
Clay City	Buckfort C. C.	9	PRI	606-663-9479
Corbin	Tri-County C. C.	9	PRI	606-528-2166
Cumberland	Sleepy Hollow C. C.	9	PRI	606-589-9381
Harlan	Harlan C. C.	9	PRI	606-573-2510
Hazard	Hazard G. C.	9	SPR	606-486-5320
Jenkins	Elkhorn C. C.	9	PRI	606-832-2118
Middlesboro	Middlesboro C. C.	9	PRI	606-248-3831
Morehead	University G. C.	9	PUB	606-783-2866
Mt. Vernon	Cedar Rapids C. C.	9	PRI	606-256-4112
Pikeville	Green Meadow C. C.	9	PRI	606-432-0712
Williamsburg	Golf and C. C.	9	PRI	606-549-2904

Other Golf Facilities

Par Threes (P3)   Executive Course (EC)

Location	Name	Holes	Type	Telephone
Allen	Stumbo Park	9	EC	606-874-2837
Ashland	Sundowner	9	P3	606-329-9093
Beattyville	Beattyville C. C.	9	EC	606-464-9286
Pineville	Pine Mountain State Resort	9	P3	606-337-6195

SOUTH CENTRAL

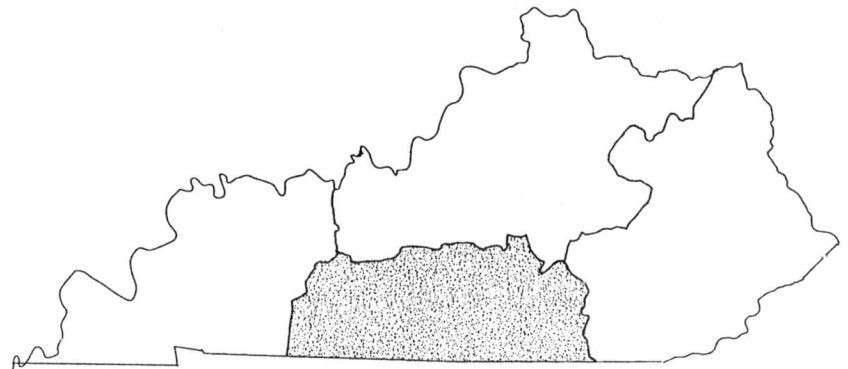

76 Falls Country Club

Route 3
Albany, Kentucky
606-387-5908

Location – Off Highway 90, 5 miles northeast of Albany.

Semi-Private	
Year Round – 9 Holes	
Manager – Tony Logan	

Greens Fees

Weekdays	$9.00
Evenings	$9.00
Weekends	$9.00

Facilities/Services Available
  Pro Shop • Driving Range •
  Putting Green •Chipping
  Green • Practice Bunker •
  Snack Bar • Dressing Rooms
  (M & W) • Private Lockers
  (M) • Golf Lessons • Group
  Play • Memberships

Rental Equipment

	9 holes	18 holes
Carts	$6.00	$10.00
Pull Carts	$1.00	$1.00

Course Description – This is an open course for the most part.
No. 5 is a generously laid out, wood-lined 489-yard dogleg
left, while the 498-yard 7th is the longest and most hazardous hole.

1991 Champions
Men's – Harvey Aaron

Tees:	Blue	White	Red
PAR:	72	72	74
Yardage:	3137	2953	2570

Bowling Green Country Club

Country Club Lane
Bowling Green, Kentucky
502-842-4581

Location – Three miles west of I-65.

Private
Year Round – 18 Holes
Golf Pro – Jeff McGill

Facilities/Services Available
Pro Shop • Driving Range •
Putting Green • Chipping Green
• Practice Bunker • Snack Bar •
Dining Room • Lounge •
Meeting Room • Dressing
Rooms (M & W) • Showers (M &
W) • Private Lockers (M & W) •
Golf Lessons • Club Repair •
Memberships

Greens Fees

	Member Guests	Guests
Weekdays	$25.00	$35.00
Evenings	$25.00	$35.00
Weekends	$25.00	$35.00

Rental Equipment

	9 holes	18 holes
Carts	$4.25	$8.50

Course Description –A feisty Buck Blankenship design encompasses all typical hazards. Gigantic 575-yard no. 5 is sprinkled with bunkers and engulfed in trees. There is a true 90-degree dogleg right on 16.

1992 Champions

Men's – Don P. Scharotin   Senior – Rhea Lazarus
Women's – Yvonne Turner   Junior – Randy Nuckols

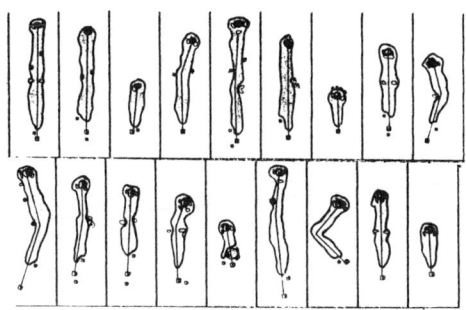

Tees:	Gold	Blue	White	Red
PAR:	72	72	72	73
Yardage:	6693	6479	6327	5400
Rating:	71.8	71.1	70.4	70.8
Slope Rating:	104	104		107

Deer Creek Golf Course

453 Rigelwood Lane
Bowling Green, Kentucky
502-782-9957

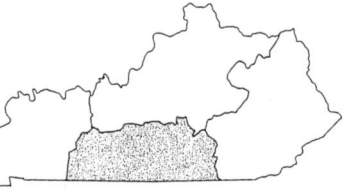

Location – U. S. 231 across Green River Parkway, first left on Brookwood, first right on Rigelwood.

Public
9 Holes
Pro – David Mahaney, PGA

Greens Fees

Weekdays	$7.00
Evenings	$4.00
Weekends	$8.00

Facilities/Services Available
Pro Shop • Putting Green •
Snack Bar • Lounge • Golf
Lessons • Club Repair •
Group Play • Memberships

Rental Equipment

	9 holes	18 holes
Carts	$8.00	$14.00
Pull Carts	$1.00	$2.00
Golf Clubs	$4.00	$6.00

Course Description – Offerings include excellent bent greens, mid-iron Bermuda tees, fescue and rye fairways. Demanding tee shots are tight, but will reward good shots. Both par 5s lay uphill and into prevailing wind – fun to play.

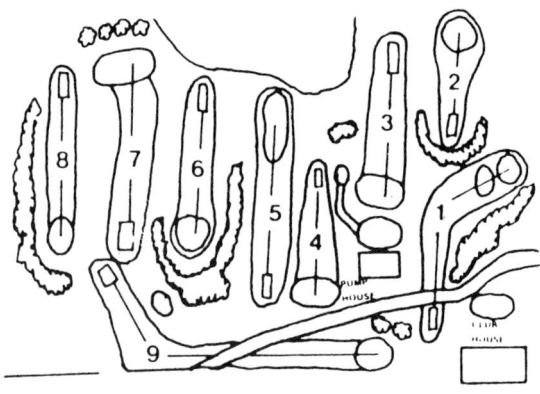

Tees:	Blue	White	Red
PAR:	36	36	36
Yardage:	3310	3020	2580
Rating:	69.9		
Slope Rating:	113	110	105

Hartland Municipal Golf Course

1031 Wilkinson Trace
Bowling Green, Kentucky
502-843-5559 or
800-786-SAND (7263)

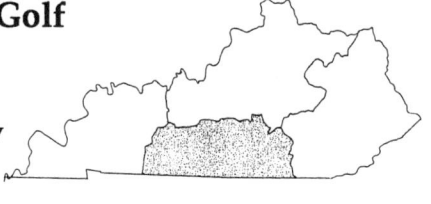

Location – Three miles east of I-65 on Route 231.

Public
Year Round – 18 Holes
Golf Course Mgr – Robert Jeffers

Greens Fees
Weekdays $12.00
Evenings $7.00
Weekends $12.00

Facilities/Services Available
Pro Shop • Putting Green •
Chipping Green • Practice
Bunker • Golf Lessons • Club
Repair • Group Play • Memberships

Rental Equipment

	9 holes	18 holes
Carts	$4.25	$8.00
Pull Carts	$1.50	$1.50
Golf Clubs	$5.00	$5.00

Course Description – Gently rolling course has large greens and plenty of sand and water.

Tees:	Blue	White	Red
PAR:	71	71	72
Yardage:	6498	5727	5044
Rating:	69.9	67.1	68.3
Slope Rating:	119	114	113

Hobson Grove Golf Course

Main Street
Bowling Green, Kentucky
502-781-2877

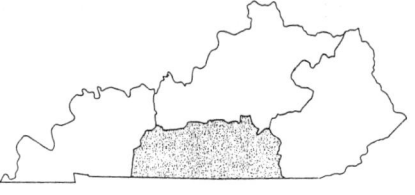

Location – Three to four miles north of downtown on Main Street.

Public
Year Round – 9 Holes
Golf Course Manager – Buck Keeton

Greens Fees
Weekdays $7.50
Weekends $8.00
Pass programs available.

Facilities/Services Available
Pro Shop • Putting Green •
Dressing Rooms (M & W) •
Golf Lessons • Club Repair •
Group Play

Rental Equipment

	9 holes	18 holes
Carts	$9.00	$15.00
Pull Carts	$1.25	$1.25
Golf Clubs	$5.00	$5.00

Course Description – Rolling fairways of medium length are topped with fast greens. Danger shouts if green is overshot on 1. High grass lines 2 and 3. Trees are a factor on most holes.

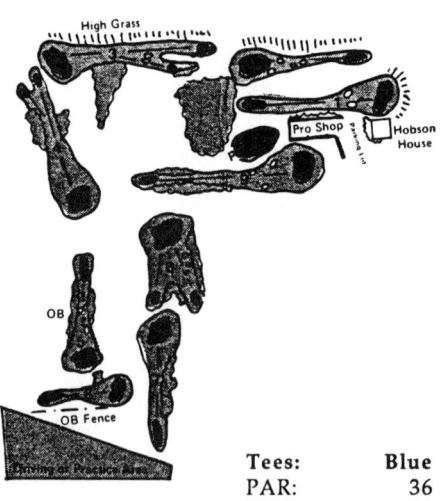

Tees:	Blue	White	Red
PAR:	36	36	37
Yardage:	3199	3106	2836

Indian Hills Country Club
200 Indian Hills Drive
Bowling Green, Kentucky
502-843-8256

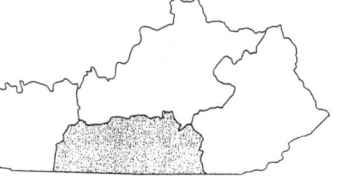

Location – I-65 and Highway 234, exit 22.

Private
Year Round – 18 Holes
Pro – Don Barber, PGA

Greens Fees Guests
Weekdays $15.00
Weekends $25.00

Facilities/Services Available
Pro Shop • Driving Range •
Putting Green • Chipping Green
• Practice Bunker • Snack Bar •
Lounge • Meeting Room •
Dressing Rooms (M & W) •
Showers (M & W) • Private
Lockers (M&W) • Golf Lessons
• Club Repair • Group Play •
Memberships

Rental Equipment

	9 holes	18 holes
Carts	$4.00	$8.00

Course Description – One of the higher slope ratings in the
state is the result of treacherous trees, narrow fairways and
small greens. Two water hazards also intensify competition.

1992 Champions
Men's – Kevin Proctor   Senior – John Beetum
Women's – Leslie Lawrence   Junior – Jon Faught

Tees:	Blue	White	Red
PAR:	71	71	72
Yardage:	6561	6139	5314
Rating:	71.5	70.7	73.2
Slope Rating:	130	126	126

Paul R. Walker Golf Course

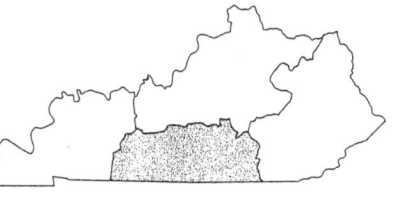

1044 Covington Avenue
Bowling Green, Kentucky
502-843-9821

Location – Three miles east of I-65 on Route 231 (Scottsville Road).

Public
Year Round –9 Holes
Pro – Buck Keeton, PGA

Greens Fees
Weekdays $7.50
Weekends $8.50
Pass program available.

Facilities/Services Available
Pro Shop • Putting Green •
Dressing Room (W) • Golf
Lessons • Club Repair •
Group Play

Rental Equipment

	9 holes	18 holes
Carts	$9.00	$15.00
Pull Carts	$1.25	$1.25
Golf Clubs	$5.00	$5.00

Course Description – This short course sports lots of mounds and mature trees. Greens are ample and fair. The straight and narrow 2nd hole is the longest, a 473-yard par 5.

Tees:	Blue	White	Red
PAR:	35	35	36s
Yardage:	3101	3012	2700
Rating:	69.4	68.6	71.2
Slope Rating:	123	122	124

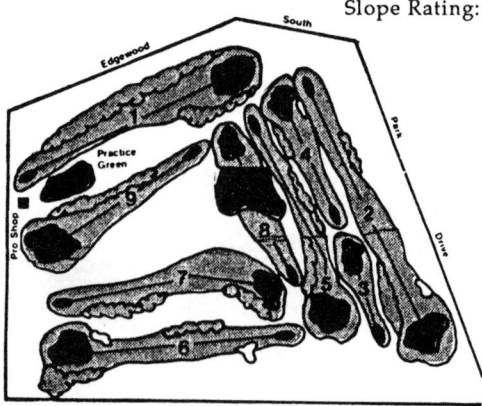

Woodson Bend Resort
Bronston, Kentucky
606-561-5316

Location – Located on Lake Cumberland

Public Resort
Year Round – 18 Holes
Pro – Tim Dudley, PGA

Greens Fees
Weekdays $22.50
Evenings $14.00
Weekends $22.50

Facilities/Services Available
Pro Shop • Driving Range •
Putting Green • Chipping
Green • Snack Bar • Golf
Lessons • Club Repair • Group
Play • Memberships

Rental Equipment

	9 holes	18 holes
Carts	$6.00	$11.50
Golf Clubs	$3.00	$3.00

Course Description – This is a beautiful, tight and challenging round of golf.

1992 Champions
Men's – Mark Eldridge
Women's – Charlotte Logsdon

Tees:	Blue	White	Red
PAR:	72	72	75
Yardage:	6189	5786	5155
Rating:	69	69	72
Slope Rating:	117	113	113

General Burnside State Park
U. S. 27
Burnside, Kentucky
606-561-4104 or 606-561-4192

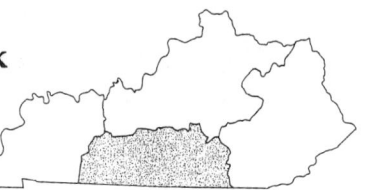

Location – Eight miles south of Somerset, Kentucky on U. S. 27.

Public
Year Round – 18 Holes
Park Manager – Sonny Hartley

Greens Fees
Weekdays $13.00
Evenings $6.50
Weekends $13.00
Kentucky State Parks pass program.

Facilities/Services Available
Pro Shop • Putting Green •
Snack Bar • Dressing Rooms
(M & W) • Showers (M & W) •
Group Play • Memberships

Rental Equipment

	9 holes	18 holes
Carts	$9.00	$17.00
Pull Carts	$2.00	$2.00
Golf Clubs	$6.00	$6.00

Course Description – Built on a 430-acre island of Lake Cumberland, this state park course offers both variety and challenge. Water interrupts the 218-yard no. 18.

Tees:	Blue	Red
PAR:	71	75
Yardage:	5905	5905
Rating:	67.5	71.6
Slope Rating:	108	107

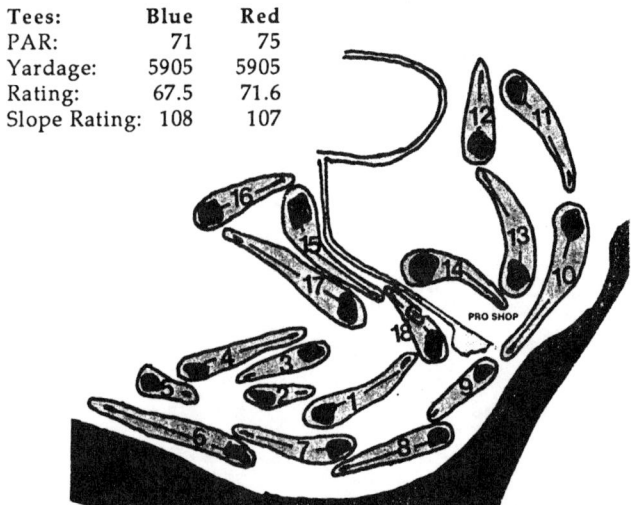

Franklin Country Club

208 Broadway
Franklin, Kentucky
502-586-6580

Private

18 Holes

Pro – Kevin Thomas, PGA

Greens Fees
Weekdays $12.00
Weekends $20.00

Facilities/Services Available
Pro Shop • Putting Green •
Chipping Green • Practice
Bunker • Snack Bar • Dining
Room • Dressing Rooms (M) •
Showers (M) • Private Lockers
(M) • Golf Lessons • Club
Repair • Group Play • Memberships

Rental Equipment

	9 holes	18 holes
Carts	$8.00	$16.00

Course Description – Trees come into play on the front nine, and a foreboding lake adds excitement on 15, 16 and 17. The dogleg left on no. 12 calls for precision placement.

1992 Champions
Men's – Brian Rohre

Tees:	Blue	Red
PAR:	71	71
Yardage:	6432	5761
Slope Rating:	116	

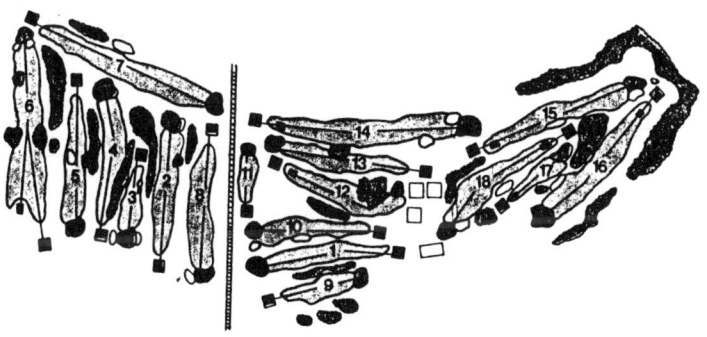

Fox Hollow Golf Club
Glasgow, Kentucky
502-678-7277

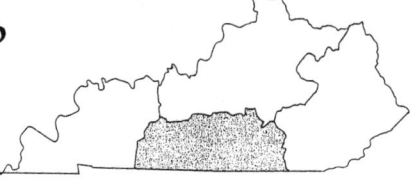

Location – One mile south of Glasgow on Hwy. 63.

Public

9 Holes

Pro – Matt Shipley, PGA

Greens Fees
Weekdays $7.50
Weekends $7.50*
*All day.
Senior discounts available.

Facilities/Services Available
Pro Shop • Driving Range •
Putting Green • Snack Bar •
Golf Lessons • Club Repair •
Group Play • Memberships

Rental Equipment

	9 holes	18 holes
Carts	$7.50	$15.00
Golf Clubs	$2.00	$4.00

Course Description – This rolling course has 2 creeks and ponds which demand accuracy. Although it has one of the lower slope ratings in the state, it plays longer because of the hills.

Tees:	Blue	Red
PAR:	71	75
Yardage:	5905	5905
Rating:	67.5	71.6
Slope Rating:	108	107

Glasgow Golf and Country Club

Glasgow, Kentucky
502-651-3955

Location – Two miles north of Glasgow on 31E.

Private
18 Holes
Pro – Doug Williams, PGA

Greens Fees
Weekdays $20.00
Weekends $20.00

Facilities/Services Available
  Pro Shop • Driving Range •
  Putting Green • Snack Bar •
  Dining Room • Lounge •
  Meeting Room • Dressing
  Rooms (M & W) • Showers
  (M & W) • Private Lockers
  (M & W) • Golf Lessons •
  Club Repair • Group Play •
  Memberships

Rental Equipment
                    18 holes
Carts $25.00

Course Description – Hills prevail to add challenge to nearly every shot.

Tees:	Blue	White	Red
PAR:	72	72	72

Green County Golf Course

Golf Course Road
Greensburg, Kentucky
606-932-7031

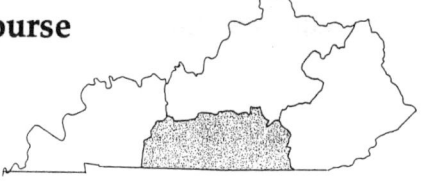

Location – Located between Campbellsville and Marshall Ridge Roads.

Private
Year Round – 9 Holes
Pro – Tim Larimore, PGA

Greens Fees
Weekdays $12.00
Evenings $12.00
Weekends $12.00

Facilities/Services Available
Driving Range • Putting Green • Snack Bar • Dining Room • Meeting Room • Dressing Rooms (M & W) • Showers (M) • Private Lockers (M & W) • Group Play • Memberships

Rental Equipment

	9 holes	18 holes
Carts	$9.00	$14.00

Course Description – This spacious layout covers rolling hills. Fine greens are large and easy to hold, but very challenging. Sand traps have recently been added throughout course.

1992 Champions
Men's – Jim Perkins

Tees:	Blue	White	Red
PAR:	36	36	37
Yardage:	3162	3150	2706

Hickory Hills Country Club
Highway 1552 (Short Town Road)
Liberty, Kentucky
606-787-7368

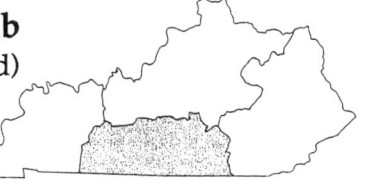

Location – Five miles north of Liberty, 1/2 mile east of U.S. 127.

Private
April thru October– 9 Holes
President – R. T. Mays

Greens Fees Guests
Weekdays $10.00
Evenings $10.00
Weekends $12.00

Facilities/Services Available
Pro Shop • Driving Range •
Putting Green • Snack Bar •
Dressing Rooms (M & W) •
Private Lockers (M & W) •
Memberships

Rental Equipment

	9 holes	**18 holes**
Carts	$6.50	$13.00

Course Description – The clubhouse overlooks rolling, picturesque, tree-lined fairways. A lake affects play on 1 - 4. No. 15 plays to an elevated, sloping, elongated green.

Tees:	Blue	White	Red
PAR:	36	36	36
Yardage:	3223	3030	2598
Rating:	70.2	67.3	66.6
Slope Rating:	112	109	106

Barren River State Resort Park

1149 State Park Road
Lucas, Kentucky
502-646-2151

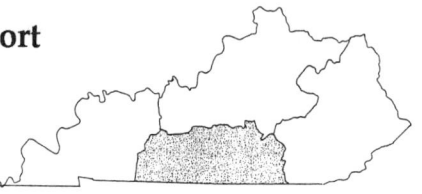

Location – Ten miles south of Glasgow on 31 E.

Public
Year Round – 9 Holes
Pro – Jimmy Bewley, PGA

Greens Fees
Weekdays $10.00
Evenings $4.50
Weekends $10.00
Kentucky State Parks pass program.

Facilities/Services Available
Pro Shop • Driving Range • Putting Green • Chipping Green • Snack Bar • Dining Room • Meeting Room • Golf Lessons • Club Repair • Group Play

Rental Equipment

	9 holes	18 holes
Carts	$8.50	$15.00
Pull Carts	$1.00	$1.00
Golf Clubs	$5.00	$5.00

Course Description – Set on a peninsula of Barren River Lake, this hilly layout has evergreen and other dense trees. The lake cuts through the 454-yard part 5 no. 4 in two places, and 9 is an extremely tight par 4.

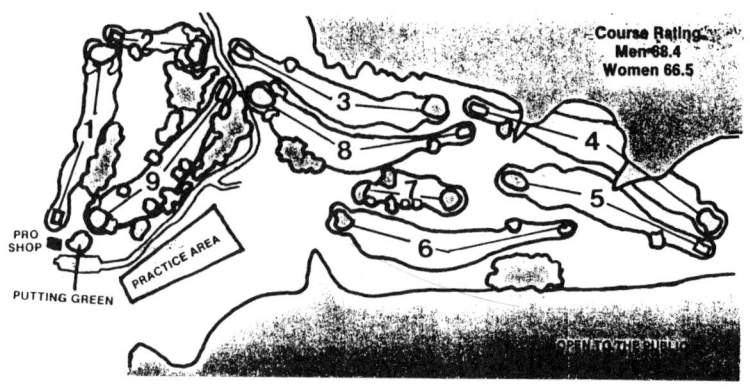

Tees:	Blue	Red
PAR:	36	35
Yardage:	2977	2290
Rating:	68.4	66.4
Slope Rating:	117	110

Monticello Country Club
400 Country Club Drive
Monticello, Kentucky
606-348-7321

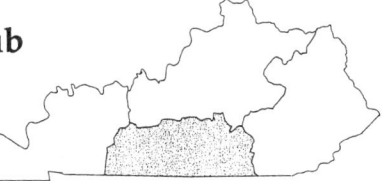

Location – On Highway 90 By-Pass.

Semi-Private
Year Round – 9 Holes
Manager – Alan Kinney, PGA

Greens Fees
Weekdays $12.00
Weekends $12.00

Facilities/Services Available
Pro Shop • Driving Range •
Putting Green • Snack Bar •
Dining Room • Dressing
Rooms (M & W) • Private
Lockers (M & W) • Golf
Lessons • Club Repair •
Group Play • Memberships

Rental Equipment

	9 holes	18 holes
Carts	$4.00	$8.00
Pull Carts	$.50	$.50

Course Description – A fairly long par 36 course, it is hilly
and has four serious doglegs. Tees overlook a lake on 8. The
483-yard no. 9 is shaped like the state of Florida with a lake
on the "Gulf Coast."

1992 Champions
Men's – Wallace Murray   Senior – Wendell Wade
        Coroy Ryan   Junior – Cory Ryan

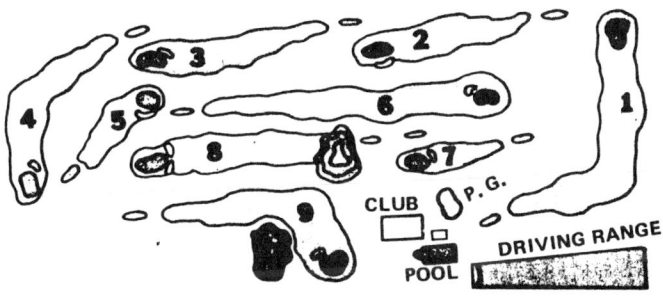

Tees:	Blue	Red
PAR:	36	39
Yardage:	3264	2771
Rating:	70.5	71.3
Slope Rating:	106	107

Breckinridge Golf & Country Club

240 Whitaker Way
Morganfield, Kentucky
502-389-3186

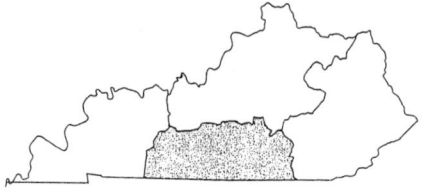

Location – One mile north of Morganfield on U.S. 60.

Semi-Private
Year Round – 9 Holes
Manager – Jack Blue

Greens Fees
Weekdays $10.00
Weekends $15.00

Facilities/Services Available
Pro Shop • Driving Range •
Putting Green • Chipping
Green • Snack Bar • Dining
Room • Lounge • Meeting
Room • Dressing Rooms (M &
W) • Showers (M & W) •Private
Lockers (M & W) • Group Play
• Memberships

Rental Equipment

	9 holes	18 holes
Carts	$8.00	$14.00
Pull Carts	Free	Free
Golf Clubs	$3.00	$3.00

Course Description – Small, elevated greens are heavily
guarded by sand. Water is a threat on six holes. Except for
three doglegs on 3, 4 and 6, holes are straight with tree-lined
fairways.

1992 Champions
Men's – Pat Lilly
Women's – Gwen Quinn

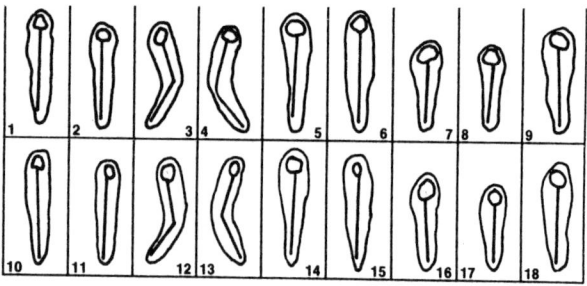

Tees:	Blue	Red
PAR:	36	37
Yardage:	2947	2706
Rating:	68.2	70.5
Slope Rating:	108	112

Park Place Resort & Golf Course

660 Doyle Road
Park City, Kentucky
502-749-9466

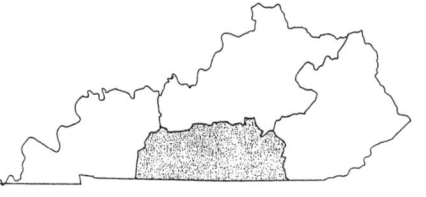

Location – Follow I-65 exit 48 toward Mammoth Cave, turn right on Doyle Road.

Public
Year Round – 18 Holes
Superintendent – Butch Cole

Greens Fees
Weekdays $10.00
Weekends $10.00
Pass program available.

Facilities/Services Available
Pro Shop • Putting Green •
Chipping Green • Practice
Bunker • Snack Bar • Dining
Room • Meeting Room •
Dressing Rooms (M & W) •
Showers (M & W) • Golf
Lessons • Group Play •
Memberships

Rental Equipment

	9 holes	18 holes
Carts	$10.00	$17.00
Golf Clubs	$6.00	$12.00

Course Description – Rolling hills make its short yardage deceiving. This is a tough but fair course.

1992 Champions
Men's – Don (Red) Brown   Senior – Henry Craine
Women's – Janice Moats   Junior – Scotty Eudy

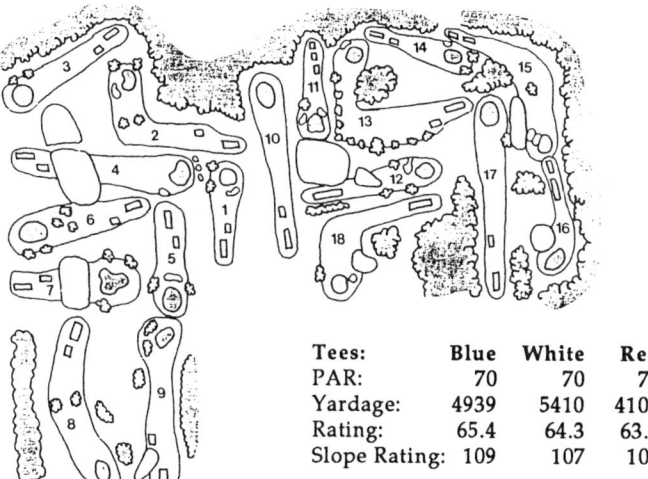

Tees:	Blue	White	Red
PAR:	70	70	70
Yardage:	4939	5410	4105
Rating:	65.4	64.3	63.4
Slope Rating:	109	107	102

Lakewood Country Club

Highway 379
Russell Springs, Kentucky
502-343-3921

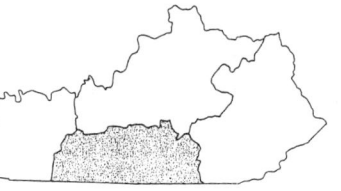

Location – Three miles from Russell Springs on Highway 379.

Semi-Private

March thru October – 18 Holes

Pro – Gregg Coe, PGA

Greens Fees
Weekdays	$10.00
Evenings	$7.00
Weekends	$12.00

Facilities/Services Available
Pro Shop • Driving Range • Putting Green • Chipping Green • Snack Bar • Dressing Rooms (M & W) • Showers (M & W) • Golf Lessons • Club Repair • Group Play • Memberships

Rental Equipment
	18 holes
Carts	$16.00
Pull Carts	$1.00
Golf Clubs	$2.00

Course Description – Rolling hills are filled with trees. Water creates a considerable danger zone on six holes. No. 15 is a tight 583-yard par 5. Bunkers add zip throughout.

Tees:	Blue	White	Red
PAR:	70	70	70
Yardage:	5870	5544	4825
Rating:	67.1	66.7	67.5
Slope Rating:	113	115	113

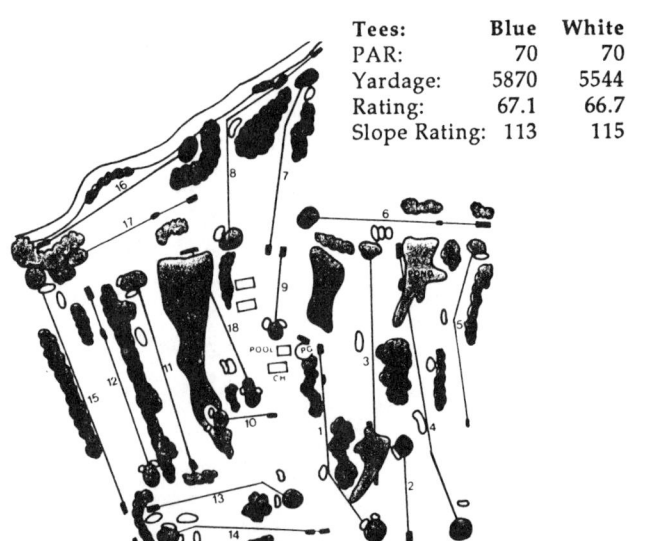

Rolling Hills Golf Course
1600 Pine Drive
Russellville, Kentucky
502-726-8700

Location – On 431 within city limits of Russellville.

Public	**Greens Fees**	
Year Round – 18 Holes	Weekdays	$9.00
Manager – Gerald McPherson	Weekends	$10.50

Facilities/Services Available
Pro Shop • Driving Range •
Putting Green • Snack Bar •
Golf Lessons • Club Repair •
Group Play

Rental Equipment

	9 holes	18 holes
Carts	$6.00	$12.00
Pull Carts	$1.00	$2.00
Golf Clubs	$1.50	$3.00

Course Description – Situated on medium rolling terrain with woods and bent grass greens.

1992 Champions
Men's – Billy Schackleford

Tees:	Blue	White	Red
PAR:	70	70	36
Yardage:	6247	6056	4874

Russellville Country Club
1710 Nashville Road
Russellville, Kentucky
502-726-7460

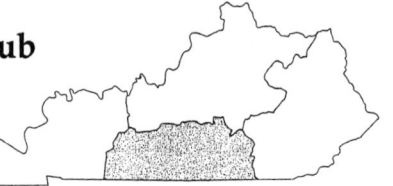

Private
9 Holes
Club Manager – Barbara Lons

Greens Fees
  with Member/Another CC
Weekdays $15.00/$20.00
Evenings $15.00/$20.00
Weekends $15.00/$20.00

Facilities/Services Available
  Pro Shop • Putting Green •
  Snack Bar • Dining Room •
  Dressing Rooms (M & W) •
  Showers (M) • Private Lockers
  (M & W)

Rental Equipment

	9 holes	18 holes
Carts	$7.50	$15.00

Course Description – Tight course has sink hole hazards! Nos. 1 and 4 are close to road, and trees make for interesting, scenic play throughout.

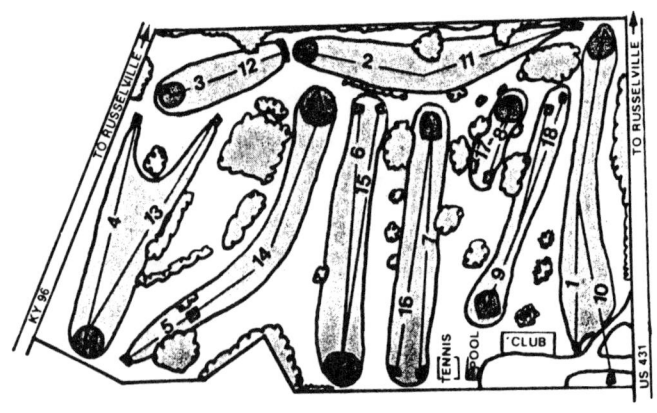

Tees:	Blue	Red
PAR:	35	36
Yardage:	3060	2792

Scottsville Country Club

Hillview Avenue
Scottsville, Kentucky
502-237-3662

Location – Twenty-five miles south of Bowling Green, Kentucky on 231.

Private
Year Round – 9 Holes

Greens Fees Guests
Weekdays $8.00
Weekends $10.00

Facilities/Services Available
Pro Shop • Putting Green •
Snack Bar

Rental Equipment

	9 holes	18 holes
Carts	$8.00	$16.00

Course Description – This short course is tight with a lot of blind shots, thanks to a hilly landscape and numerous trees. It has only one water hazard.

Tees:	Blue	White	Red
PAR:	35	35	37
Yardage:	2659	2576	2526
Rating:	69.6	64.6	68.1
Slope Rating:	114	114	117

Eagle's Nest Country Club

Highway 39N
Somerset, Kentucky
606-679-7754

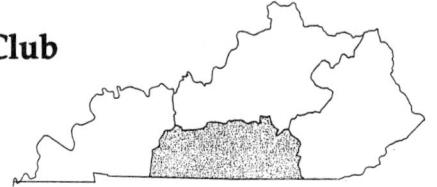

Location – Three miles north of Highway 80.

Private	
Year Round – 18 Holes	
Pro – Greg Flesher, PGA	

Greens Fees Guests
Weekdays $21.00
Weekends $21.00

Facilities/Services Available
 Pro Shop • Driving Range •
 Putting Green • Snack Bar •
 Dining Room • Meeting Room
 • Dressing Rooms (M & W) •
 Showers (M & W) • Private
 Lockers (M & W) • Golf
 Lessons • Club Repair •
 Memberships

Rental Equipment

	9 holes	18 holes
Carts	$8.00	$16.00
Golf Clubs	$5.00	$5.00

Course Description – The slick, well-maintained greens are only half the battle on this challenging course that contains water, woods and bunkers on most holes. It's a golfing test for players of all abilities.

1992 Champions
Men's – Happy Rakestran
Women's – Sandy Stokley

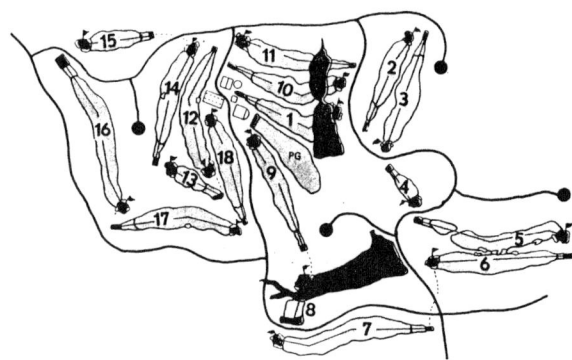

Tees:	Blue	White	Red
PAR:	71	71	72
Yardage:	6404	6224	5152
Rating:	70.6	69.1	72.6
Slope Rating:	119	113	109

Slate Branch Golf Course

1077 Slate Branch Road
Somerset, Kentucky
606-679-3113

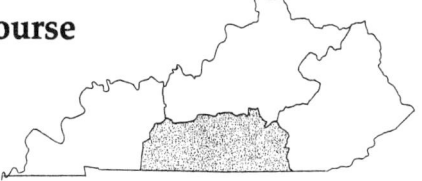

Location – 7/10 mile west of Highway 27 on Highway 1642.

Public

Year Round – 18 Holes

Owner – Tim Lair

Greens Fees
Weekdays $12.00
Weekends $12.00

Facilities/Services Available
Pro Shop

Rental Equipment

	9 holes	18 holes
Carts	$4.00	$8.00

Course Description – Major water hazards on 6 holes add chills to a course that tests both long and short skills.

Tees:	Blue	White	Red
PAR:	71	71	71
Yardage:	6090	5827	4699
Rating:	68.7	67.5	66.3
Slope Rating:	117	114	109

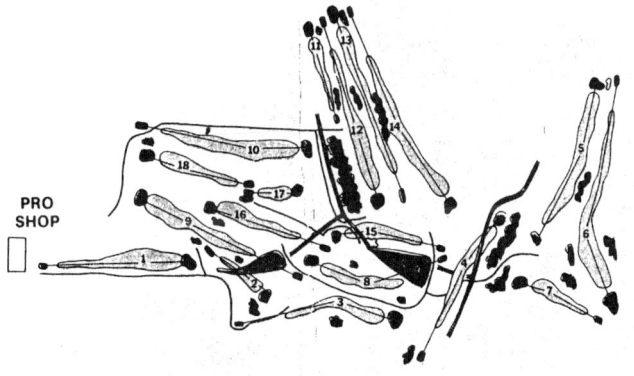

PRO
SHOP

Stearns Golf Course
Park Road
Stearns, Kentucky
606-376-2666

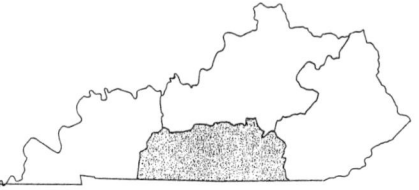

Location – One-quarter mile from downtown Stearns.

Semi-Private	
Year Round – 9 Holes	

Greens Fees
Weekdays $8.00
Evenings $8.00
Weekends $8.00

Facilities/Services Available
Pro Shop • Putting Green •
Chipping Green • Snack Bar •
Dining Room • Club Repair •
Group Play • Memberships

Rental Equipment

	9 holes	18 holes
Carts	$6.00	$12.00
Pull Carts	$.50	$1.00

Course Description – This short field is set on gently rolling hills. Trees and shrubbery add to difficulty as do two water hazards.

Tees:	Blue	Red
PAR:	35	37
Yardage:	2859	2463
Rating:	66.3	66.8
Slope Rating:	103	104

Hidden Hills Golf & Country Club
Golf Course Road
Tompkinsville, Kentucky
502-487-8172

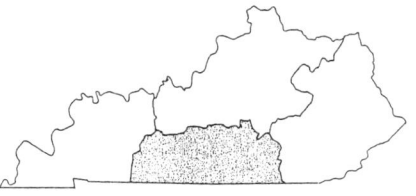

Location – Follow 163 east 3 blocks to Mill Creek Road for 1/2 mile.

Semi-Private	
Year Round – 9 Holes	
Pro – Danny Crowder, PGA	

Greens Fees

Weekdays	$10.00
Evenings	$10.00
Weekends	$15.00

Facilities/Services Available
Pro Shop • Driving Range •
Putting Green • Chipping
Green • Snack Bar • Meeting
Room • Showers (M & W) •
Golf Lessons • Club Repair •
Group Play • Memberships

Rental Equipment

	9 holes	18 holes
Carts	$4.50	$14.00

Course Description – Although only one hole has water, lakes outline most of the course. Three major doglegs are found on three holes, while two others curve slightly.

1992 Champions
Men's – Michael Carter   Junior – Amy Crowder
Women's – Phyllis Pitcock

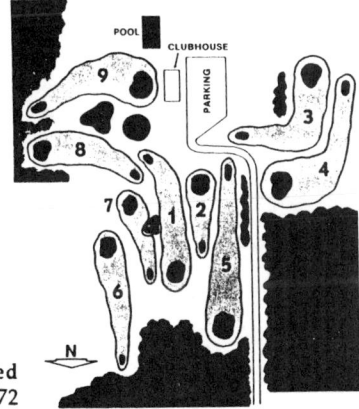

Tees:	Blue	White	Red
PAR:	72	72	72
Yardage:	3018	3008	2998
Rating:	70.3	69.3	71.9
Slope Rating:	118	116	119

SOUTH CENTRAL APPENDIX

Additional Regulation Courses

Location	Name	Holes	Type	Telephone
Campbellsville	Campbellsville C.C.	18	PRI	502-789-1670
Columbia	Pinewood C.C.	9	PRI	502-384-3613
Horse Cave	Caveland C.C.	9	PRI	502-786-9905
Jamestown	Lake Cumberland State Resort	9	PUB	502-343-3111
Morgantown	Hidden Valley G. C.	9	PUB	502-526-4643
Somerset	Somerset C.C.	9	PRI	606-678-4623

Other Golf Facilities

Executive Course (EC)   Practice Range (PR)

Location	Name	Holes	Type	Telephone
Bowling Green	Otte Golf Center	–	PR	502-781-6072
Park City	Park Mammoth Resort	18	EC	502-749-4101

WESTERN REGION

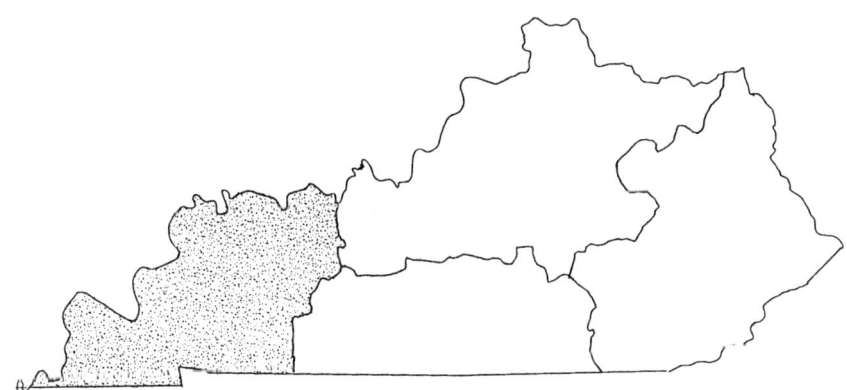

Lake Barkley State Resort Park

Blue Springs Road
Cadiz, Kentucky
502-924-9076

Location – Four miles west of Cadiz on Highway 68.

Public
Year Round – 18 Holes
Pro – Bill Love, PGA

Greens Fees

Weekdays	$15.00
Evenings	$7.50
Weekends	$15.00

Kentucky State Parks pass program.

Facilities/Services Available
Pro Shop • Driving Range • Putting Green • Chipping Green • Snack Bar • Dining Room • Lounge • Meeting Room • Dressing Rooms (M & W) • Showers (M & W) • Golf Lessons • Club Repair • Group Play

Rental Equipment

	9 holes	18 holes
Carts	$9.00	$17.00
Pull Carts	$1.00	$2.00
Golf Clubs	$6.00	$6.00

Course Description –Also known as the Boots Randolph Golf Course, this lush layout winds through two valleys along a creek bed. Big Blue Spring, stocked with rainbow trout, feeds the creek that adds interest throughout the course. A stream bisects 12 and 18.

1992 Champions

Men's – Jackie Sholar	Senior – Emil Locher
Women's – Jamie Towler	Junior – Lori Gray

Tees:	Blue	White	Red
PAR:	72	72	72
Yardage:	6751	6448	5477
Rating:	71.5	70.1	70.3
Slope Rating:	131	125	121

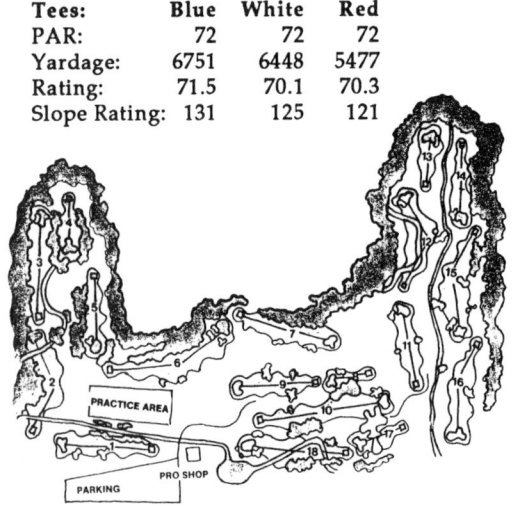

Calvert City Golf & Country Club

Country Club Lane
Calvert City, Kentucky
502-395-5831

Location – One and one-half miles off I-24 Calvert City exit.

Semi-Private	
Year Round – 18 Holes	
Manager – Karen Freeman	

Greens Fees
Weekdays $15.00
Weekends $25.00

Facilities/Services Available
Pro Shop • Driving Range •
Putting Green • Practice
Bunkder • Snack Bar •
Lounge • Dressing Rooms (W)
• Showers (W) • Private
Lockers (W) • Club Repair •
Group Play

Rental Equipment

	9 holes	18 holes
Carts	$7.45	$14.90
Pull Carts		$1.00

Course Description –Major components include wide, tree-lined Bermuda fairways. While sand is found on six holes, water makes its presence known on seven.

1992 Champions
Men's – Brandon Larimer   Senior – John Davis
Women's – Karen Puckett

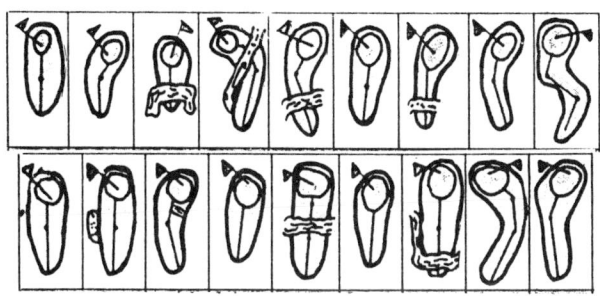

Tees:	Blue	White	Red
PAR:	72	72	72
Yardage	6762	6507	5486
Rating	70.3	69.1	69.3
Slope Rating:	111	108	109

Oak Hill Recreation

Clinton, Kentucky
502-653-6001

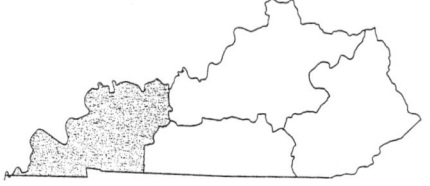

Location – One mile north of Clinton on Highway 51.

Public
9 Holes
Manager – Tom Roberts

Greens Fees
Weekdays $8.00
Weekends $12.00

Facilities/Services Available
Pro Shop • Putting Green •
Chipping Green • Snack Bar •
Memberships

Rental Equipment

	9 holes	18 holes
Carts	$8.00	$16.00

Course Description – The challenge here includes a long par 3 on no. 7 and interesting dogleg right on no. 5.

1992 Champions
Men's – Todd Johnson
Women's – Liz Myers

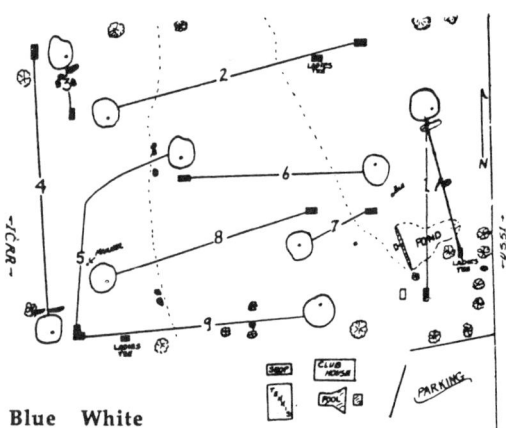

Tees:	Blue	White
PAR:	36	35
Yardage:	2956	2906
Rating:	67.5	67.5

Pennyrile Forest State Resort Park

Kentucky 109
Dawson Springs, Kentucky
502-797-3421

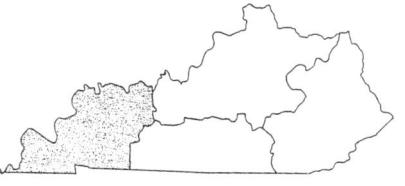

Location – Eight miles south of Dawson Springs on Kentucky 109.

Public Resort
Year Round – 9 Holes
Pro Shop Supervisor – Sam Jones

Greens Fees
Weekdays $10.00
Evenings $10.00
Weekends $10.00
Kentucky State Parks pass program.

Facilities/Services Available
Pro Shop • Putting Green •
Snack Bar • Dining Room •
Lounge • Meeting Room •
Group Play

Rental Equipment

	9 holes	18 holes
Carts	$9.00	$17.00
Pull Carts	$2.00	$2.00
Golf Clubs	$6.00	$6.00

Course Description – One of the best 9-hole courses in the Kentucky State Park system is fairly flat and extremely well-conditioned. The par 5 no. 3 is the most rigorous hole, with a 75-yard uphill shot to the green.

Tees:	Blue	White	Red
PAR:	36	36	36
Yardage:	3405	3270	3058

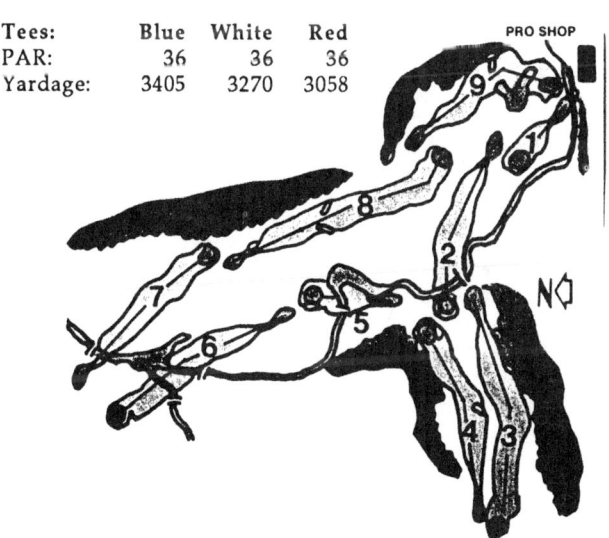

PRO SHOP

Lakeside Municipal Golf Course

Highway 973
Dunmore, Kentucky
502-657-8260

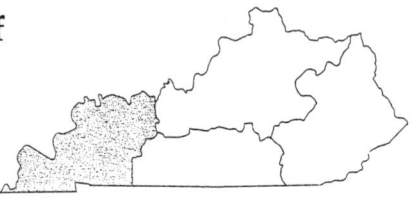

Location – Two miles from Lake Malone State Park off Highway 431.

Public
Year Round – 9 Holes
Owner/Manager – Ed Mallory

Greens Fees Guests
Weekdays $3.50
Weekends $4.50

Facilities/Services Available
  Pro Shop • Driving Range •
  Putting Green • Snack Bar •
  Club Repair • Group Play

Rental Equipment

	9 holes	18 holes
Carts	$5.50	$11.00
Pull Carts	$1.00	
Golf Clubs	$1.00	

Course Description – Hazards are everywhere in the form of water and ditches, intermixed with trees.

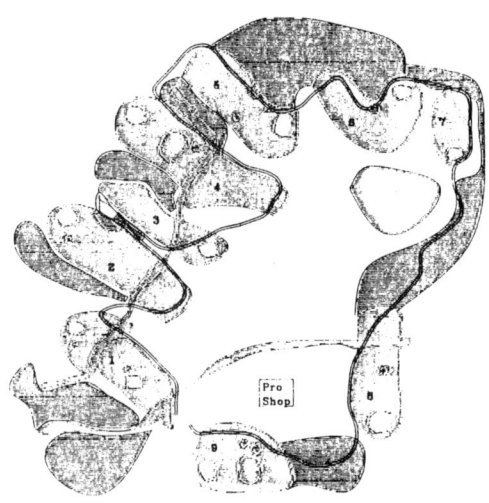

Tees:	Blue	White	Red
PAR:	35	34	35
Yardage:	2877	2612	2155

Elk Fork Country Club
Jefferson Street
Elkton, Kentucky
502-265-5340

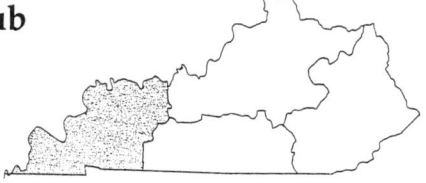

Location – West Jefferson, Elkton.

Private
Year Round – 9 Holes
Manager – Paul Hampton

Greens Fees Guests
Weekdays $5.00
Weekends $10.00

Facilities/Services Available
  Driving Range • Putting
  Green • Snack Bar •Private
  Lockers (M)

Rental Equipment

	9 holes	18 holes
Carts	$5.00	$10.00

Course Description – Contoured for interest and versatility, this is a flat course. Second hole stretches to 560 yards and gives little latitude for mistakes. No. 9 is another narrow par 5, 470-yard dogleg left.

1992 Champions
Men's – Kevin Harris
Women's – Libby Ross

Tees:	Blue	Red
PAR:	36	36
Yardage:	3136	2812
Rating:	69.6	72.0

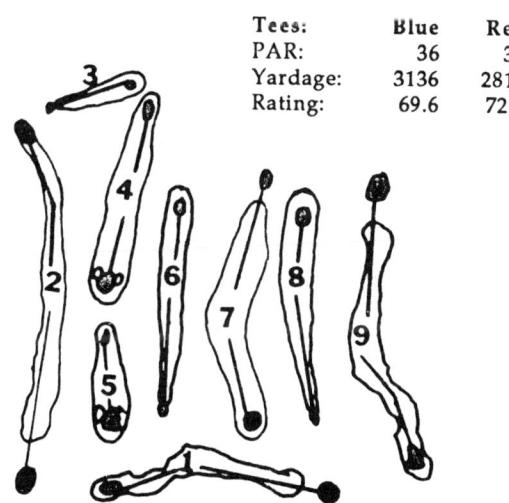

Kentucky Dam Village State Resort Park

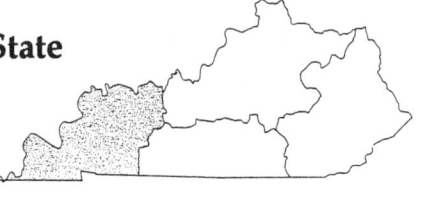

Highway 641
Gilbertsville, Kentucky
502-362-4271 or 502-362-8658

Location – Two miles east of I-24 on U.S. Highway 641.

Public	
Year Round – 18 Holes	
Pro – Steve Perryman, PGA	

Greens Fees
Weekdays $15.00
Evenings $7.50
Weekends $15.00
Kentucky State Parks pass program.

Facilities/Services Available
Pro Shop • Driving Range •
Putting Green • Dining Room
• Meeting Room • Group Play
• Memberships

Rental Equipment

	9 holes	18 holes
Carts	$9.00	$17.00
Pull Carts	$2.00	$2.00
Golf Clubs	$6.00	$6.00

Course Description – This wooded course is fair, but tests skills at all levels. Eight holes stretch beyond 400 yards, with 18 being the grandaddy of them all, a 546-yard dogleg right.

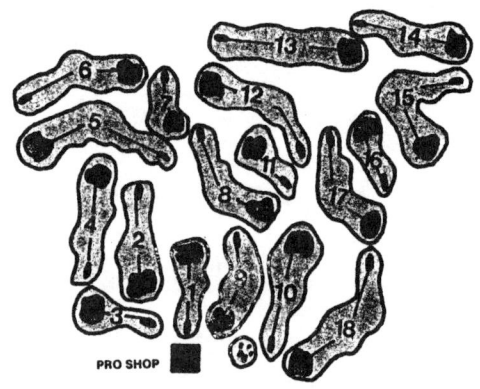

PRO SHOP

Tees:	Blue	White	Gold	Red
PAR:	72	72	72	72
Yardage:	6704	6307	5839	5094
Rating:	73.0	71.0		70.1
Slope Rating:	135	131		124

Greenville Country Club

Greenville, Kentucky
502-338-3233

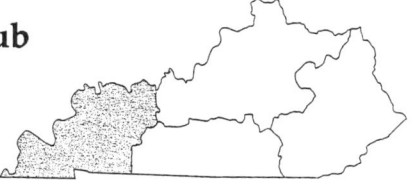

Location – Two miles south of Greenville on Rt. 181 S.

Semi-Private	**Greens Fees**
Summer Only – 9 Holes	Weekdays $10.00
Manager – Brenda Wade	Weekends $15.00

Facilities/Services Available
  Pro Shop • Driving Range
  • Putting Green • Snack Bar •
  Dining Room • Lounge •
  Meeting Room • Dressing
  Rooms (M & W) • Golf Lessons
  • Club Repair • Group Play •
  Memberships

Rental Equipment

	9 holes	18 holes
Carts	$5.00	$10.00
Pull Carts	$1.00	$1.00

Course Description – Large lake is the dominant feature of this short but challenging course.

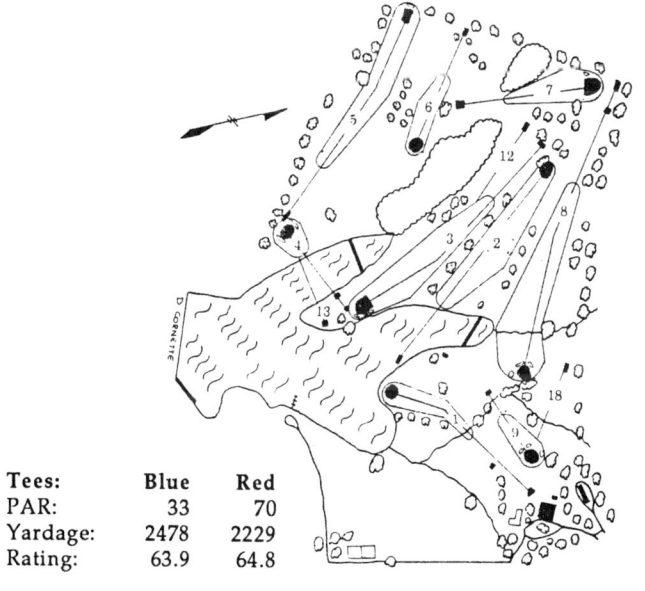

Tees:	Blue	Red
PAR:	33	70
Yardage:	2478	2229
Rating:	63.9	64.8

Twin Oak Golf Course
Greenville, Kentucky
502-338-4653

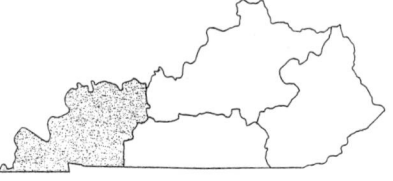

Location – One-half mile west of Greenville on Route 62.

Public
Year Round – 9 Holes
Manager – Dennis Linker

Greens Fees
Weekdays $6.00
Weekends $16.00
Winter rates available.

Facilities/Services Available
Pro Shop • Putting Green •
Chipping Green • Snack Bar •
Lounge • Dressing Rooms (M
& W) • Golf Lessons • Club
Repair • Group Play • Mem-
berships

Rental Equipment

	9 holes	18 holes
Carts	$5.00	$8.00
Pull Carts	$2.00	$4.00
Golf Clubs	$2.00	$2.00

Course Description – Very hilly, and challenging, every hole
has a major water threat!

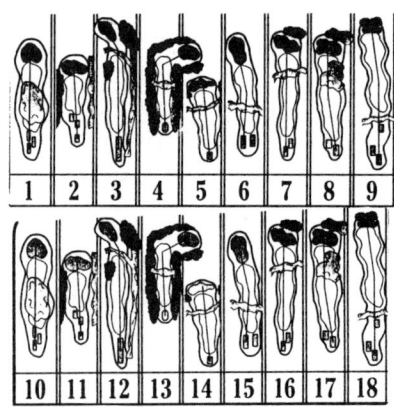

Tees:	Blue	White	Red
PAR:	35	35	36
Yardage:	2863	2693	2351

Ohio County Country Club
Country Club Road
Hartford, Kentucky
502-298-7210

Location – One mile south of U.S. 69 near Green River Parkway.

Private	
April thru October – 9 Holes	

Greens Fees Guests
Weekdays $7.00
Weekends $8.00

Facilities/Services Available
Driving Range • Putting
Green • Snack Bar • Dining
Room • Dressing Rooms (M) •
Group Play • Memberships

Course Description – Rolling terrain, trees, out of bounds and small, elevated greens place a premium on accuracy rather than length.

Tees:	Blue	Red
PAR:	35	37
Yardage:	2793	2585
Rating:	66.3	68.9
Slope Rating:	109	113

Windward Heights Country Club

Highway 271 South
Hawesville, Kentucky
502-927-6603

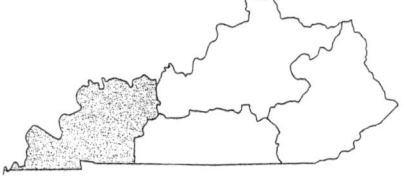

Location – Quarter mile off U.S. 60 between Hawesville and
Lewisport on Highway 271 South.

Private
April thru October – 9 Holes
Club Manager – Terry Griffin

Greens Fees
Weekdays $10.00
Weekends $15.00
American Lung Association
Cards accepted.

Facilities/Services Available
Pro Shop • Putting Green •
Snack Bar • Dressing Rooms (M
& W) • Showers (M & W) •
Private Lockers (M & W) • Golf
Lessons • Club Repair • Group
Play • Memberships

Rental Equipment

	9 holes	18 holes
Carts	$8.00	$16.00
Pull Carts	$1.00	$1.00

Course Description – This medium-length course is built on a
rolling landscape with two tee sets for 18 holes. Tree-lined
fairways are fairly wide and the greens are ample. Water
interrupts 6 and 7.

1992 Champions
Men's – Terry Griffin
Women's – Karen Brown

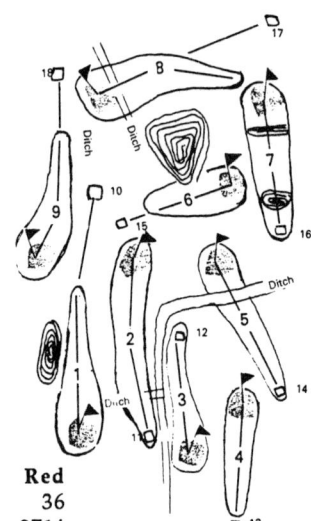

Tees:	Blue	White	Red
PAR:	36	36	36
Yardage:	3102	2788	2714
Rating:	67.8	66.2	70.4
Slope Rating:	117	114	119

Henderson Country Club
1030 Country Club Drive
Henderson, Kentucky
502-827-3444
Location – On Highway 60 East.

Private
March thru December – 18 Holes
Pro – Ron Reiner, PGA

Greens Fees Guests
Weekdays $33.00*
Weekends $33.00*
*Includes cart.

Facilities/Services Available
Pro Shop • Driving Range •
Putting Green • Chipping Green
• Practice Bunker • Snack Bar •
Dining Room • Lounge •
Meeting Room •Dressing Rooms
(W) • Showers (M & W) •
Private Lockers (M & W) • Golf
Lessons • Club Repair • Group
Play • Memberships

Rental Equipment

	9 holes	**18 holes**
Carts	$8.00	$16.00

Course Description – A mighty layout includes tight, tree-lined fairways and much sand. Water constitutes a major obstacle on four holes, and will consume misplayed balls on two others. Back nine is rigorous.

1992 Champions
Men's – Darryl Wayne
Women's – Patty Reed

Senior – Jack McDonald
Junior – Jack Bugg

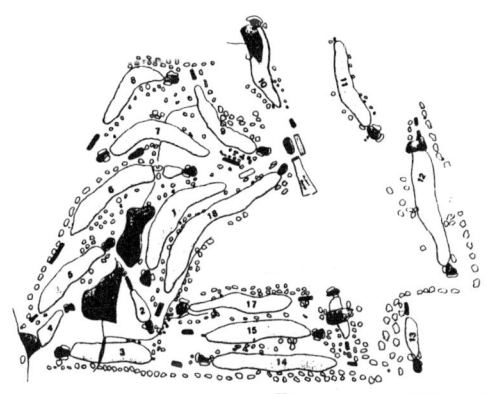

Tees:	Blue	White	Red
PAR:	72	72	72
Yardage:	6655	6136	5274
Rating:	71.8	69.1	70.2
Slope Rating:	130	124	123

Henderson Municipal Golf Course

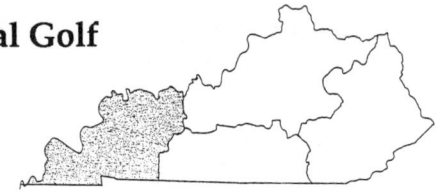

1801 North Elm Street
Henderson, Kentucky
502-831-1263

Location – Two blocks from 41N Strip.

Public
Year Round – 9 Holes
Manager – Jerry Church

Greens Fees

	9 Holes	18 Holes
Weekdays	$4.00	$6.00
Weekends	$5.00	$7.00

Pass programs available.

Facilities/Services Available
Pro Shop • Snack Bar • Golf Lessons • Group Play • Memberships

Rental Equipment

	9 holes	18 holes
Carts	$7.00	$12.00
Pull Carts	$1.50	$2.25
Golf Clubs	$5.00	$5.00

Course Description – Bunkers have recently been added to all holes on this short, hilly course. Fairways are tight and lined with trees.

1992 Champions
Men's – Jimmy Watkins
Women's – Joyce Gill

Water Tower ➜ ◯

Club House

Tees:	Blue	White	Red
PAR:	32	32	34
Yardage:	1981	1981	
Rating:	57.5	60.4	

John James Audubon State Park

U. S. Highway 41 North
Henderson, Kentucky
502-826-5546

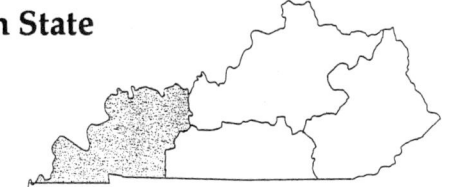

Location – One mile south of Henderson/Evansville, Indiana Bridge.

Public
Year Round – 9 Holes
Manager – Jim Chapman

Greens Fees
Weekdays $10.00
Evenings $8.00
Weekends $10.00
Kentucky State Parks pass program.

Facilities/Services Available
Pro Shop • Driving Range •
Putting Green • Snack Bar •
Golf Lessons • Club Repair •
Group Play • Memberships

Rental Equipment

	9 holes	18 holes
Carts	$9.00	$17.00
Pull Carts	$2.00	$4.00
Golf Clubs	$6.00	$6.00

Course Description – Set in the scenic hills of western Kentucky in Audubon State Park, it provides a good challenge for all abilities.

1992 Champions
Men's – Darrel Wayne   Senior – Roy Lawson
Women's Helen Clark

Tees:	Blue	White	Red
PAR:	36	36	38
Yardage:	3360	3120	2900
Rating:	69.5	68.7	69.2
Slope Rating:	113	111	111

Hickman Country Club

Route 1
Hickman, Kentucky
502-236-9128

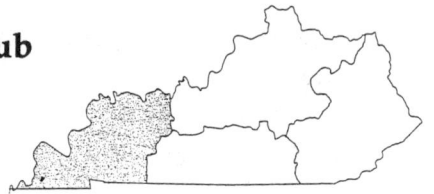

Location – One and one-half miles south of town on Highway 125.

Private	
March thru October – 9 Holes	
Manager – Richard Wilkerson	

Greens Fees Guests
Weekdays $10.00
Weekends $10.00

Facilities/Services Available
  Pro Shop • Putting Green •
  Snack Bar • Dining Room •
  Lounge • Meeting Room

Rental Equipment

	9 holes	18 holes
Carts	$6.00	$12.00

Course Description – This short course is tree lined with only a few hazards. Must be accurate with driver on 2, 7 and 9 as ditches come into play. Sand traps on 1, 2, 5, and 6. Bermuda greens are excellent. Birdies can be made here, but must keep ball in fairway.

1992 Champions
Men's – Rick Childers
Women's – Cindy Terrett

Tees:	Blue	Red
PAR:	36	37
Yardage:	3079	2750

Hopkinsville Golf & Country Club

303 Country Club Lane
Hopkinsville, Kentucky
502-886-2498

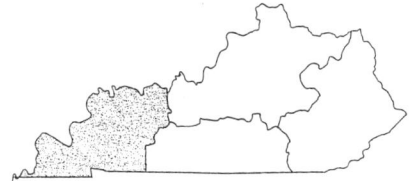

Location – One mile west of 41A.

Private	**Greens Fees** Guests
Year Round – 18 Holes	Weekdays $15.00
Pro – Blake Spicer, PGA	Weekends $25.00

Facilities/Services Available
Pro Shop • Driving Range •
Putting Green • Snack Bar •
Dining Room • Lounge •
Dressing Rooms (M & W) •
Showers (M & W) • Private
Lockers (M & W) • Golf
Lessons • Club Repair •
Memberships

Rental Equipment

	9 holes	18 holes
Carts	$8.00	$15.00

Course Description – The well-bunkered, hilly course has recently changed from Bermuda to bent grass greens. Fairways are lined with trees, and there are no water hazards.

1992 Champions
Men's – Rusty Nunn   Senior – Jerry McRae
Women's – Ann Young

Tees:	Blue	White	Red
PAR:	71	71	72
Yardage:	6414	6106	5092
Rating:	69.6	66.8	68.9
Slope Rating	119	114	115

Skyline Golf Course
Skyline Drive
Hopkinsville, Kentucky
502-885-0943

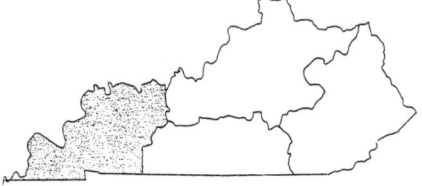

Location – Off Highway 41A, 1-1/2 miles south of Hopkinsville.

Public

Year Round – 9 Holes

President – Elliott Miles

Greens Fees
Weekdays $8.00
Evenings $6.00
Weekends $10.00
Pass program available.

Facilities/Services Available
Pro Shop • Driving Range •
Putting Green • Practice
Bunker • Snack Bar • Private
Lockers (M & W) • Club Repair
• Group Play

Rental Equipment

	9 holes	18 holes
Carts	$7.50	$14.00
Pull Carts	$4.00	$4.00
Golf Clubs	$5.30	$5.30

Course Description – This 9-hole course has long par 3s and a 600-yard par 5. Fairways are narrow.

1992 Champions
Men's – Elliott Miles

Tees:	Blue	Red
PAR:	36	36
Yardage:	3075	3075
Rating:	66.9	72.1
Slope Rating:	105	115

Tijeras Creek Golf Course
Highway 68 East
Hopkinsville, Kentucky
502-885-6023

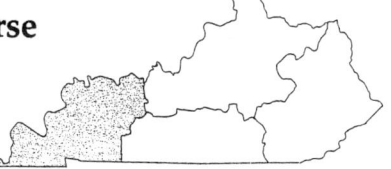

Location – Highway 68 E, Pennyrile Parkway exit 9, toward Russellville.

Public
Year Round – 18 Holes
Pro – Jim Jones, PGA

Greens Fees
Weekdays $11.00
Weekends $13.00
Pass programs available.
American Lung Association
Card accepted.

Facilities/Services Available
  Pro Shop • Driving Range •
  Putting Green • Dressing
  Rooms (W) • Golf Lessons •
  Club Repair • Group Play •
  Memberships

Rental Equipment

	9 holes	18 holes
Carts	$8.00	$16.00

Course Description –Formerly Western Hills, this course presents numerous dangers. Water plays prominently on five holes and is a lateral hazard on four others. Sand is strategically-placed throughout.

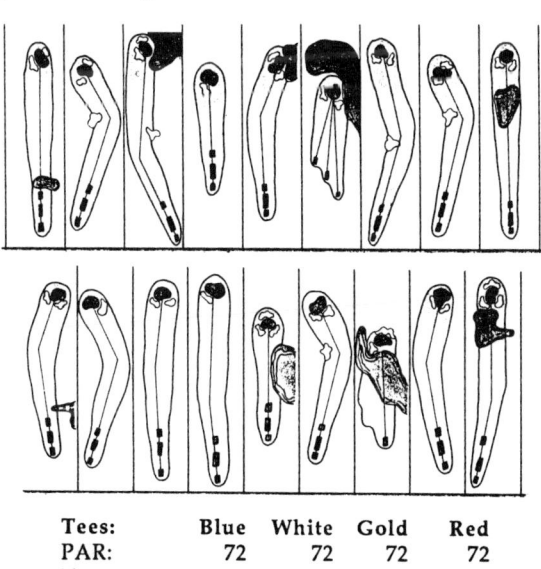

Tees:	Blue	White	Gold	Red
PAR:	72	72	72	72
Yardage:	6907	6455	5586	3919
Rating:	73.8	71.8	67.8	64.0
Slope Rating:	134	130	122	109

Ballard Country Club
Rt. 1
LaCenter, Kentucky
502-665-9992

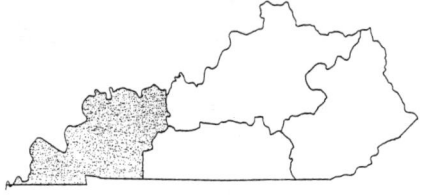

Location – Twenty miles west of Paducah on 802 at LaCenter.

Semi-Private	
18 Holes	
Pro – Barry Faulkner, PGA	

Greens Fees Guests
Weekdays $12.00
Weekends $14.00

Facilities/Services Available
Pro Shop • Driving Range •
Putting Green • Chipping
Green • Practice Bunker •
Snack Bar • Golf Lessons •
Club Repair • Group Play •
Memberships

Rental Equipment

	9 holes	18 holes
Carts	$8.00	$15.00
Pull Carts	$1.00	$1.00

Course Description – Wide open with rolling hills and ponds on front. Back nine heavily wooded and challenging, narrow with lots of water.

1992 Champions
Men's – Gary Chandler

Tees:	Blue	Red
PAR:	72	72
Yardage:	6154	4953
Rating:	69.0	68.9
Slope Rating:	114	112

Lakeshore Country Club
Shamrock Drive
Madisonville, Kentucky
502-821-2069

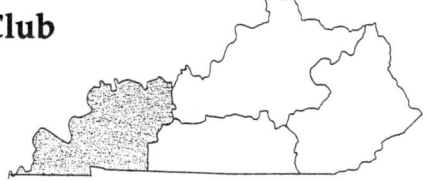

Location – One and one-half miles off U.S. 41.

Private		
April thru December – 9 Holes		
Pro – Cyrus Britt, PGA		

Greens Fees Guests
Weekdays $10.00
Evenings $10.00
Weekends $15.00

Facilities/Services Available
Pro Shop • Driving Range •
Putting Green • Chipping
Green • Snack Bar •Dining
Room • Lounge • Meeting
Room • Golf Lessons • Club
Repair • Group Play •
Memberships

Rental Equipment

	9 holes	18 holes
Carts	$7.00	$14.00
Pull Carts	$2.00	$1.00
Golf Clubs	$5.00	$5.00

Course Description – This scenic course is hilly and inundated with a wide variety of trees. Three water hazards stiffen the friendly challenge.

Tees:	Blue	White	Red
PAR:	36	36	36
Yardage:	3100	2700	2000
Rating:	70.7	69.7	67.7
Slope Rating:	111	109	106

Madisonville City Golf Course

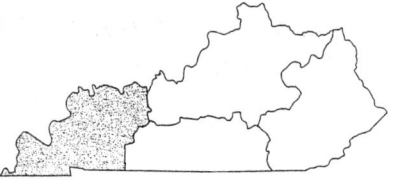

755 Park Road
Madisonville, Kentucky
502-824-2156

Location – From downtown, left on Broadway, then right on Park Road.

Public	
Year Round – 18 Holes	
Superintendent – Mike Franklin	

Greens Fees
Weekdays $6.00
Evenings $6.00
Weekends $6.00
Pass programs available.

Facilities/Services Available
Pro Shop • Driving Range •
Putting Green • Snack Bar •
Meeting Room • Golf Lessons
• Club Repair • Group Play

Rental Equipment

	9 holes	18 holes
Carts	$7.00	$14.00

Course Description – Golfers face slim fairways, trimmed with trees and sand traps galore. Eight holes are divided by water, calling for solid, consistent strategy in playing this medium length course.

1992 Champions
Men's – Bill Knopp   Junior – Curtis Massey

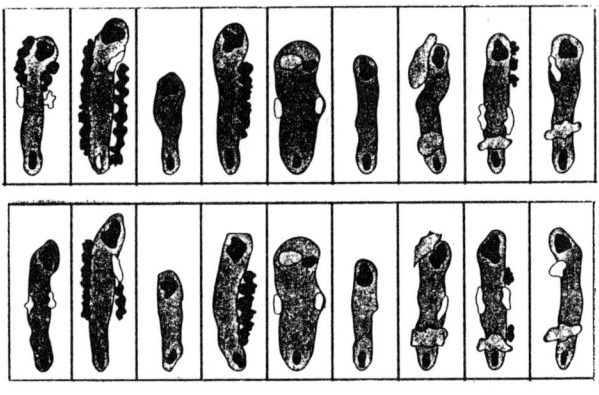

Tees:	Blue	Red
PAR:	70	70
Yardage:	5871	4640
Rating:	69.4	72.4
Slope Rating:	111	101

Madisonville Country Club

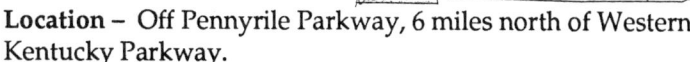

Country Club Lane
Madisonville, Kentucky
502-821-3700

Location – Off Pennyrile Parkway, 6 miles north of Western Kentucky Parkway.

Private	**Greens Fees** Guests
Year Round – 18 Holes	Weekdays $15.00
Pro – Mike Thomas, PGA	Weekends $25.00

Facilities/Services Available
Pro Shop • Driving Range •
Putting Green • Chipping Green
• Practice Bunker • Snack Bar •
Dining Room • Lounge •
Meeting Room • Dressing
Rooms (M & W) • Showers (M &
W) • Private Lockers (M) • Golf
Lessons • Club Repair •
Memberships

Rental Equipment

	9 holes	18 holes
Carts	$9.00	$16.00

Course Description – This is a fascinating open design which includes midiron Bermuda fairways and patches of pampas grass. A two-forked creek intersects five holes, and ponds are foreboding on four more. Sand must be maneuvered around on all holes.

1992 Champions
Men's – Phil Thomas
Women's – Sharon Fuller

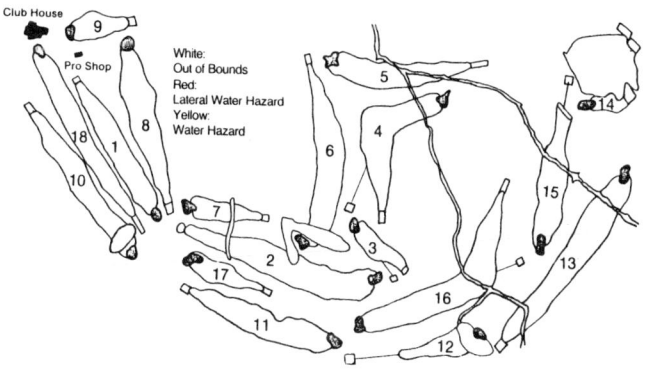

Tees:	Blue	White	Red
PAR:	71	72	72
Yardage:	6574	6273	5141
Rating:	70.8	68.9	68.7
Slope Rating:	124	121	116

Marion Country Club
South Blackburn Street
Marion, Kentucky
502-965-9241

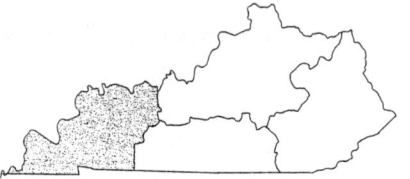

Location – Approximately 1/4 mile off Highway 60 W.

Semi-Private
Year Round – 9 Holes
Superintendent – Dwayne Croft

Greens Fees

Weekdays	$10.00
Evenings	$10.00
Weekends	$14.00

Facilities/Services Available
Pro Shop • Putting Green •
Snack Bar • Dining Room •
Dressing Rooms (M) •
Showers (M) • Group Play
• Memberships

Rental Equipment

	9 holes	18 holes
Carts	$8.00	$14.00

Course Description – Game is challenged by rolling hills and trees that are everywhere. A creek runs across four fairways, creating hazards. Bent greens are small on this extra tough course.

1992 Champions
Men's – Butch Jepson   Senior – Russell Nelson

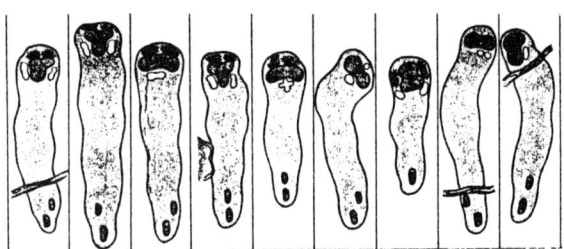

Tees:	Blue	White	Red
PAR:	36	36	39
Yardage:	3177	3099	2570
Rating:	70.6	69.6	63.6
Slope Rating:	128	126	114

Mayfield Golf & Country Club

West Broadway
Mayfield, Kentucky
502-247-1862

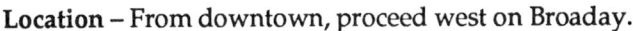

Location – From downtown, proceed west on Broaday.

Private	
Year Round – 18 Holes	
Pro – Mary Offutt, PGA	

Greens Fees Guests
Weekdays $18.00
Evenings $18.00
Weekends $18.00

Facilities/Services Available
Pro Shop • Driving Range • Putting Green • Practice Bunker • Snack Bar • Lounge • Meeting Room • Dressing Rooms (M & W) • Showers (M & W) • Private Lockers (M & W) • Club Repair • Group Play • Memberships

Rental Equipment

	9 holes	18 holes
Carts	$8.00	$14.00

Course Description – The site of several KGA championships and the West Kentucky Amateurs has unforgiving fairways. Water winds throughout as lateral hazards. The difficult layout is contoured around a variety of obstacles.

1992 Champions
Men's – Darren Hillis
Women's – Sandy Weintraub

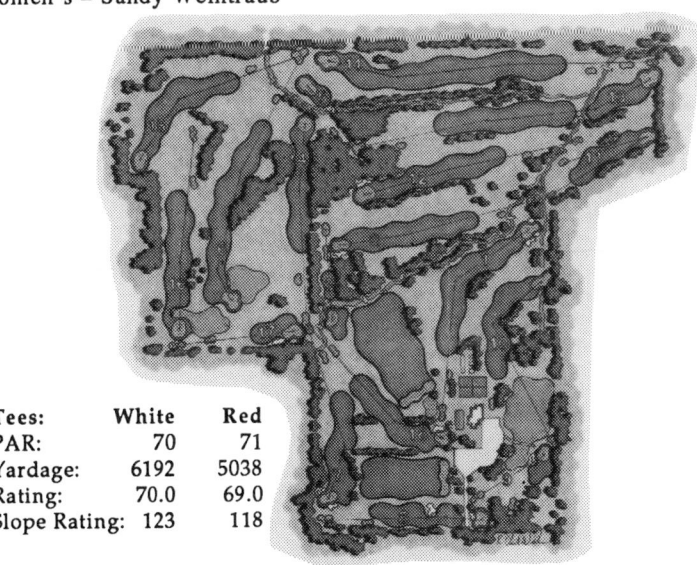

Tees:	White	Red
PAR:	70	71
Yardage:	6192	5038
Rating:	70.0	69.0
Slope Rating:	123	118

Miller Memorial Golf Course
Route 6
Murray, Kentucky
502-762-2238

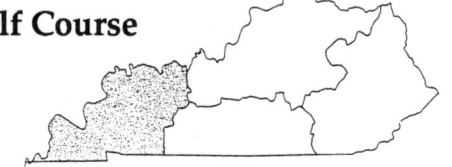

Location – Five miles east of Murray on Highway 280, off Highway 94E.

Public
Year Round – 18 Holes
Pro – Raymond Hewitt

Greens Fees
Weekdays $14.00
Evenings $7.00
Weekends $14.00
Pass program available.
American Lung Association
Cards accepted.

Facilities/Services Available
Pro Shop • Driving Range •
Putting Green • Chipping
Green • Snack Bar •Golf
Lessons • Club Repair •
Group Play • Memberships

Rental Equipment

	9 holes	18 holes
Carts	$8.00	$16.00
Pull Carts	$2.00	$2.00
Golf Clubs	$6.00	$6.00

Course Description – The American Society of Golf Architects lists this among the Top 130 Best Designed Courses in the United States. Wide Bermuda fairways are capped with large, rolling bent grass greens. Three lakes and sand add zest to the test.

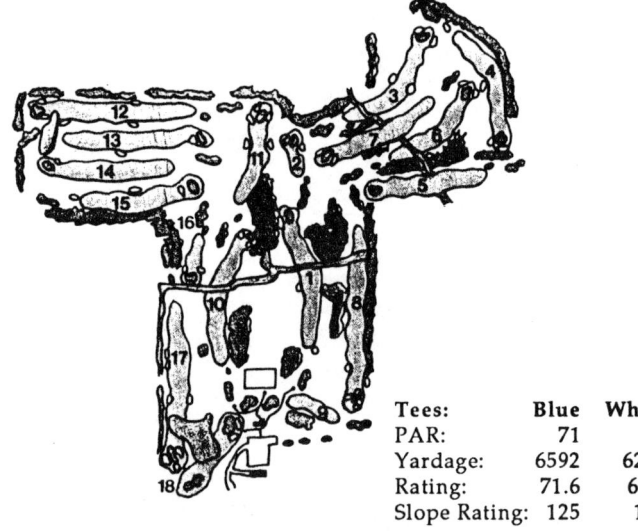

Tees:	Blue	White	Red
PAR:	71	71	71
Yardage:	6592	6229	5058
Rating:	71.6	69.9	68.9
Slope Rating:	125	122	117

Murray Country Club

College Farm Road
Murray, Kentucky
502-753-9430

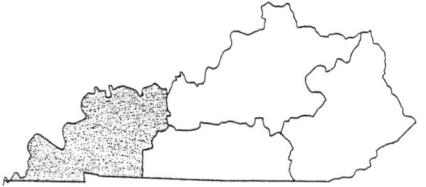

Location – In town, follow Main west to 18th and turn right, to College Farm Road, turn left; 1/2 mile on right.

KGA – Private	Greens Fees Guests	
	Weekdays	$20.00
Year Round – 18 Holes	Evenings	$10.00
Pro – Tom Schwettman , PGA	Weekends	$20.00

Facilities/Services Available
Pro Shop • Driving Range •
Putting Green • Chipping
Green • Practice Bunker •
Snack Bar • Dining Room •
Meeting Room • Dressing
Rooms (M & W) • Showers (M)
• Private Lockers (M & W) •
Golf Lessons • Club Repair •
Memberships

Rental Equipment

	9 holes	18 holes
Carts	$7.00	$14.00
Pull Carts		$1.00

Course Description – A flat arena, with the biggest hazard on this course, large trees and water on 4, 9, 13, and 16. Although there are few bunkers, a heavy rough can play havoc.

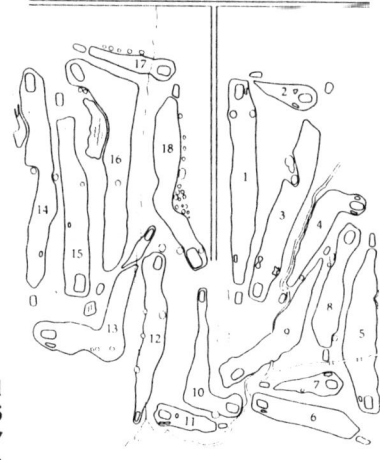

MURRAY COUNTRY CLUB

Tees:	Blue	White	Red
PAR:	72	72	75
Yardage:	6304	6025	5397
Rating:	70.2		69.9
Slope Rating:	115		115

Ben Hawes State Park
400 Booth-Field Road
Owensboro, Kentucky
502-684-9808

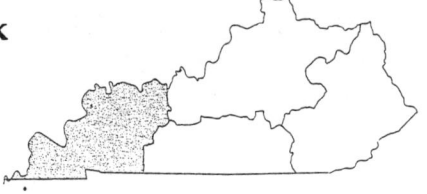

Location – Two miles west of Owensboro, off Highway 60W.

Public	
Year Round – 18 Holes	
Pro – Nick Madison	

Greens Fees
Weekdays	$10.00
Evenings	$5.00
Weekends	$10.00

Facilities/Services Available
Pro Shop • Driving Range •
Putting Green • Chipping
Green • Snack Bar • Golf
Lessons

Rental Equipment
	9 holes	18 holes
Carts	$9.00	$16.00
Pull Carts	$1.00	$1.00
Golf Clubs	$5.00	$5.00

Course Description –The front nine on this course is flat, while the back nine is hilly. Bermuda fairways and bent grass greens are well-conditioned. Seven holes have water hazards.

Tees:	Blue	White	Red
PAR:	71	71	76
Yardage:	6591	6372	5371
Rating:	71.0	71.0	70.0
Slope Rating:	118	116	115

Summit Country Club

6501 Summit Drive
Owensboro, Kentucky
502-281-0000

Private
18 Holes
Director of Golf – Drew Augenstein

Greens Fees Guests
Weekdays $25.00
Weekends $30.00

Facilities/Services Available
Pro Shop • Driving Range •
Putting Green • Chipping
Green • Practice Bunker •
Snack Bar •Dining Room •
Lounge • Meeting Room •
Dressing Room (M & W) •
Showers (M & W) • Private
Lockers (M & W) • Golf Lessons
• Club Repair • Group Play •
Memberships

Rental Equipment

	9 holes	18 holes
Carts	$4.00	$6.00
Golf Clubs	$7.50	$15.00

Course Description – This new course is open to the public for a limited period before it will become private. Call first.

Tees:	Gold	Blue	Red	Senior
PAR:	72	72	72	72
Yardage:	6616	6169	5121	5563

Village Green Golf Course
427 Highway 554
Owensboro, Kentucky
502-785-4565

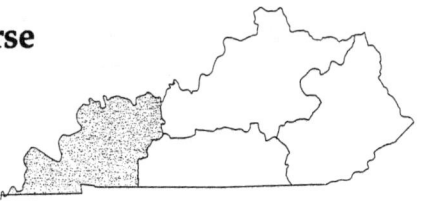

Location – In Utica, 4 miles west of Highway 81.

Public

Year Round – 9 Holes

Manager – Keith Lambrick

Greens Fees
Weekdays $5.00

Facilities/Services Available
Pro Shop • Putting Green •
Chipping Green • Snack Bar •
Lounge • Dressing Rooms (M
& W) • Showers (M & W) •
Group Play • Memberships

Rental Equipment

	9 holes	18 holes
Carts	$9.00	$15.00
Pull Carts	$1.00	
Golf Clubs	$5.00	

Course Description – Gently rolling hills have moderately-wide fairways with elevated greens for added difficulty. Three small lakes comes into play on 1, 8, and 9. The secluded location provides scenic quiet.

Tees:	Blue	White	Red
PAR:	34	34	37
Yardage:	2965	2876	2875
Rating:	69.2	72.8	70.6
Slope Rating:	120	116	118

Windridge Country Club
5044 Millers Mill Road
Owensboro, Kentucky
502-685-3639

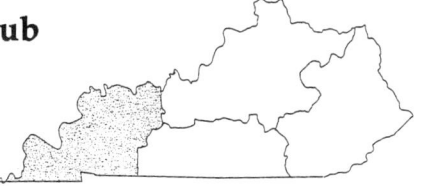

Location – Southeast of U.S. 231.

Private	
Year Round – 18 Holes	

Greens Fees Guests
Weekdays $16.00
Weekends $20.00

Facilities/Services Available
Pro Shop • Driving Range •
Putting Green • Chipping
Green • Dining Room •
Lounge • Meeting Room •
Showers (M) • Private Lockers
(M) • Memberships

Rental Equipment

	9 holes	18 holes
Carts	$10.00	$18.00

Course Description – The terrain is hilly and sand is plentiful. Trees surround the course, and water challenges par scoring on eight holes.

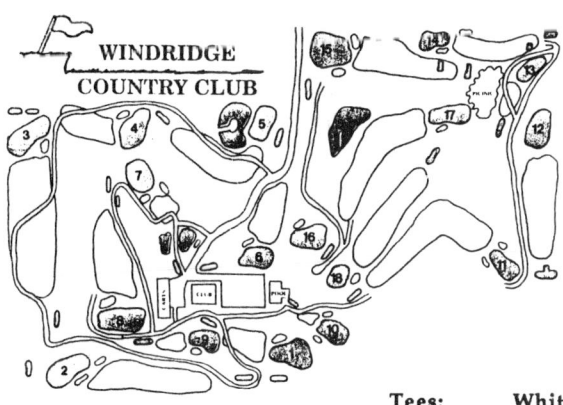

Tees:	White	Red
PAR:	71	71
Yardage:	5951	5737
Rating:	67.2	71.7
Slope Rating:	115	118

Country Club of Paducah
6500 Turnberry Drive
Paducah, Kentucky
502-554-5330

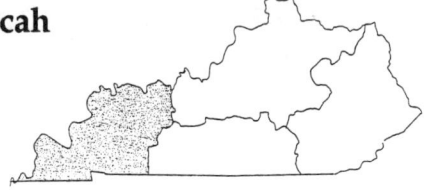

Private

18 Holes

Pro – A. Todd Trimble, PGA

Facilities/Services Available
Pro Shop • Driving Range • Putting
Green • Chipping Green • Practice
Bunker • Snack Bar • Dining Room
• Lounge • Meeting Room • Dress-
ing Rooms (M) • Showers (M) •
Pivate Lockers (M) • Golf Lessons •
Club Repair • Group Play • Mem-
berships

Course Description – The Country Club of Paducah is a Robert
Trent Jones design and currently ranked 4th in the state by
Golf Week.

1992 Champions

Men's – Jim Brown   Senior – Vito Canonico
Women's – Monica Kim   Junior – Ward Davis

Tees:	Blue	White	Red
PAR:	72	72	72
Yardage:	6800	6363	5341
Rating:	72.9	71.1	70.5
Slope Rating:	130	127	122

Paxton Park Golf Course

841 Berger Road
Paducah, Kentucky
502-444-9514

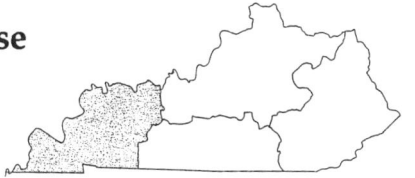

Location – U.S. 45N from I-24, about one mile down Berger Road.

	Greens Fees	
Public	Weekdays	$9.50
Year Round – 18 Holes	Weekends	$9.50
Park Director – Daniel "Kayo" Mullen		

Facilities/Services Available
Pro Shop • Driving Range •
Putting Green • Snack Bar •
Dressing Rooms (M & W) •
Showers (M & W) • Private
Lockers (M & W) • Golf Lessons • Club Repair • Group
Play

Rental Equipment

	18 holes
Carts	$14.00
Pull Carts	$2.50
Golf Clubs	$3.25

Course Description – A rolling to moderately hilly course has direct patterns to greens. Trees line and interrupt medium fairways. The par 5 no. 9 extends to 606 yards, while 6 is a 90-degree, 348 yard dogleg right.

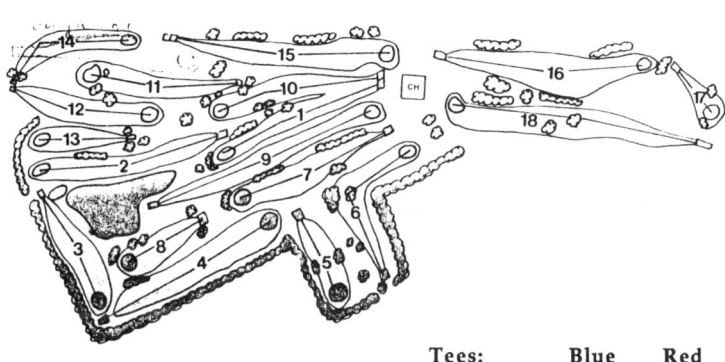

Tees:	Blue	Red
PAR:	71	76
Yardage:	6536	5762
Rating:	70.9	70.2
Slope Rating:	117	116

Rolling Hills Country Club
700 Lake View Drive
Paducah, Kentucky
502-554-9054

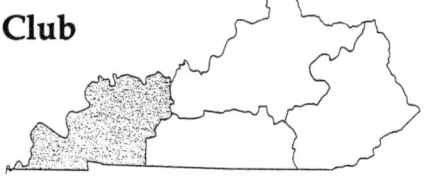

Location – One-half mile off Highway 45S.

Private Year Round – 18 Holes

Greens Fees Guests
Weekdays $15.00
Evenings $15.00
Weekends $15.00

Facilities/Services Available
  Pro Shop • Putting Green •
  Snack Bar • Lounge • Dress-
  ing Rooms (M & W) • Showers
  (M & W) • Private Lockers (M &
  W) • Golf Lessons • Group
  Play • Memberships

Rental Equipment

	9 holes	18 holes
Carts	$6.00	$12.00

Course Description –Fairways zig zag through trees on a
rolling landscape. No. 9 is a 504-yard double dogleg right
and left, and 15 is a straight and narrow 569-yard par 5.

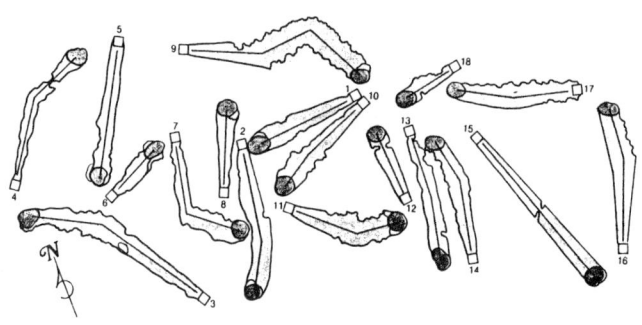

Tees:	Blue	White	Red
PAR:	71	71	74
Yardage:	6072	6013	5092
Rating:	69.0		68.9
Slope Rating:	114		112

Westwood Country Club
Country Club Lane
Paducah, Kentucky
502-444-9811

Location – In Paducah, follow Pines Road to Country Club Lane.

Private

Year Found – 9 Holes

Greens Fees Guests
Weekdays $12.00
Weekends $15.00

Facilities/Services Available
Pro Shop • Putting Green •
Snack Bar • Dining Room •
Dressing Rooms (M & W) •
Showers (M & W) • Private
Lockers (M & W) • Golf
Lessons

Rental Equipment

	9 holes	18 holes
Carts	$6.00	$12.00

Course Description – Numerous sand traps toughen this par 36 course. Fairways allow little leeway. Mature trees line all paths.

Tees:	Blue	Red
PAR:	36	36
Yardage:	2560	2939
Rating:	67.5	68.5
Slope Rating:	118	117

Paintsville Country Club
Country Club Road
Paintsville, Kentucky
606-789-4234

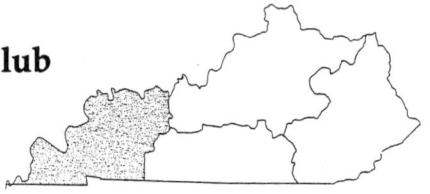

Location – From Paintsville Route 23, follow Route 40 east
to Route 1107 (Country Club Road).

Private	**Greens Fees** Guests
Year Round – 18 Holes	Weekdays $10.00
	Evenings $6.50
Pro – Luther Conley, PGA	Weekends $12.50

Facilities/Services Available
Pro Shop • Putting Green •
Snack Bar • Dining Room •
Lounge • Meeting Room •
Dressing Rooms (M & W) •
Showers (M & W) • Private
Lockers (M & W) • Golf Lessons
• Club Repair • Group Play •
Memberships

Rental Equipment

	9 holes	18 holes
Carts	$8.00	$15.00
Pull Carts	$1.00	$2.00
Golf Clubs	$2.00	$5.00

Course Description – Nos. 10 and 17 are played over the Big
Sandy River, which golfers cross on 155-yard swinging
bridge. Four other water hazards are part of the hilly layout.
Trees trim tight fairways.

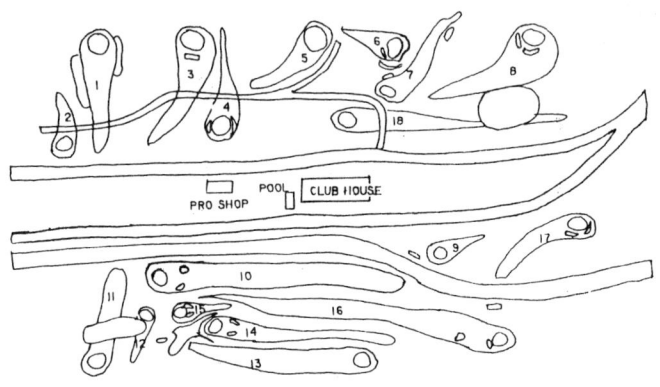

Tees:	Blue	White	Red
PAR:	70	70	74
Yardage:	6370	5500	5184
Rating:	65.5	65.4	78.0
Slope Rating:	110	106	108

WESTERN APPENDIX

Additional Regulation Courses

Location	Name	Holes	Type	Telephone
Benton	Benton Golf and C.C.	9	PRI	502-427-9673
Central City	Central City C.C.	9	PRI	502-754-4312
Mayfield	South Highland C.C.	18	PRI	502-247-2918
Murray	Oaks C.C.	18	PRI	502-753-6454
Owensboro	Hillcrest G.C.	9	PUB	502-685-8353
Owensboro	Owensboro C.C.	18	PRI	502-683-3387
Princeton	Princeton Golf and C. C.	18	PRI	502-365-6110
Providence	Providence Golf and C. C.	9	PRI	502-667-5027

Other Golf Facilities

Par Threes (P3)   Executive Course (EC)

Location	Name	Holes	Type	Telephone
Gilbertsville	Mr. Golf	9	P3	502-362-8239
Hardin	Kenlake State Resort	9	EC	502-474-2211
Henderson	Municipal Golf Course	9	P3	502-831-1263
Murray	Pinnacle	9	P3	502-753-1152

Course Index

City Index

Rough River 117
Russell Springs 158
Russellville 159-60

S

Scottsville, 161
Shelbyville 102-3, 117
Shepherdsville 104, 117
Somerset 162-63, 166
Springfield 105
Stanford 106
Stearns 164

T

Taylorsville 107
Tompkinsville 165

U

Union 108

V

Valley Station 109, 117
Versailles 110-11
Vine Grove 112

W

Warsaw 113
West Liberty 136
Wheatley 114
Williamsburg 137
Winchester 11-17